MORE
RIPPING YARNS

By the same authors:

Ripping Yarns
Bert Fegg's Nasty Book for Boys and Girls

MORE
RIPPING YARNS

MICHAEL PALIN AND TERRY JONES

ART DIRECTION & DESIGN: KATE HEPBURN

PHOTOGRAPHS: BERTRAND POLO & AMO

METHUEN

Whinfrey's Last Case: First transmitted on BBC-2 October 10th 1979

Directed by Alan J.W. Bell; *Photographed by* Alan Stevens and Mike Radford;
Edited by Glenn Hyde; *Designed by* Gerry Scott; *Sound Recordists* Ron Blight and Ron Pegler;
Dubbing Mixer Ron Edmonds; *Costume Designer* Roger Reece; *Make-Up Artist* Jill Hagger;
Visual Effects John Horton; *Graphics Designer for the series* Ian Hewitt
Production Assistants John Adams and Sue Bennett-Urwin; *Director's Assistant* Carol Abbott;
Assistant Sound Recordist Morton Hardaker; *Grips* Malcolm Sheehan;
Assistant Designer Alan Spalding; *Property Buyer* Enid Willey; *Lighting Gaffer* Ricky Wood;
Make-Up Assistant Caroline Becker; *Assistant Floor Manager* Julie Mann;
Assistant Film Editor Brian Douglas; *Design Assistant* Sarah Leigh
Cast: *Introducer, Whinfrey* Michael Palin; *Meat Lorry Driver* Steve Conway;
General Chapman Jack May; *Lord Raglan* Gerald Sim; *Admiral Jefferson* Antony Carrick;
Man in club Anthony Woodruff; *Barmaid (Lotte)* Ann Way; *Mrs Otway* Maria Aitken;
Mr Carne Richard Hurndall; *Mr Ferris* Charles McKeown; *Mr Girton* Edward Hardwicke;
Mr Vinney Patrick Bailey; *Smooth German* Michael Sharvell-Martin;
Another Eddie Philip Clayton-Gore; *Army Captain* Roy Sampson; *Germans* Members of
the Royal Marines, Exmouth

Filmed on location in London; Torbryan, Devon; Staverton Bridge, Devon (Dart Valley Railway);
Cape Cornwall; and at the BBC Television Film Studios, Ealing

Golden Gordon: First transmitted on BBC-2 October 17th 1979

Directed by Alan J.W. Bell; *Photographed by* Alan Stevens; *Edited by* John Jarvis;
Designed by Gerry Scott; *Sound Recordist* Ron Blight; *Dubbing Mixer* Ron Edmonds;
Costume Designer Roger Reece; *Make-Up Artist* Jill Hagger; *Visual Effects* John Horton;
2nd Unit Cameraman Michael Radford;
Production Assistants John Adams and Sue Bennett-Urwin; *Director's Assistant* Carol Abbott
Assistant Sound Recordist Morton Hardaker; *Assistant Designer* Alan Spalding;
Prop Buyer Enid Willey; *Lighting Gaffer* Ricky Wood; *Grips* Malcolm Sheehan;
Assistant Cameraman Steve Albins; *Assistant Costume Designer* Sarah Leigh;
Assistant Film Editor Christine Pancott; *Make-up Assistant* Caroline Becker
Cast: *Mrs Ottershaw* Gwen Taylor; *Barnstoneworth Ottershaw* John Berlyne;
Gordon Ottershaw Michael Palin; *Barman (Cyril)* Ken Kitson; *Football Manager* David Leland;
1st Footballer David Ellison; *2nd Footballer* Colin Bennett; *3rd Footballer* Matthew Scurfield;
Chairman Teddy Turner; *Arthur Foggen* Bill Fraser; *Mrs Foggen* Pat Taylor;
Baldy Davitt Roger Sloman; *Goalkeeper* Charles McKeown; *Passer-by* John Cleese;
and members of Salts A.F.C. (who didn't mind having their hair cut)
Filmed entirely on location in Keighley (the Ottershaw home), Kildwick (the Foggen home),
Saltaire, Bradley, Bingley and Guiseley in Yorkshire

Roger of the Raj: First transmitted on BBC-2 October 24th 1979

Directed by Jim Franklin; *Photographed by* Reg Pope; *Edited by* Dan Rae;
Designed by Nigel Curzon; *Sound Recordist* Bob Roberts; *Dubbing Mixer* Alan Dykes;
Costume Designer Valerie Bonner; *Make-up Artist* Cecile Hay-Arthur;
Production Assistant Peter R. Lovell; *Producer's Assistant* Elizabeth Cranston;
Visual Effects Designer John Horton; *Assistant Floor Manager* John Bishop;
Design Assistant Richard Brackenbury; *Costume Assistant* Tessa Hayes;
Make-Up Assistant Margaret Magee; *Property Buyer* Eric Baker;
Assistant Cameraman Richard Gauld; *Sound Assistant* John Corps; *Grips* Tex Childs;
Lighting Gaffer Ted Bird; *Assistant Film Editor* Arden Fisher
Cast: *Roger* Michael Palin; *Lord Bartlesham* Richard Vernon; *Lady Bartlesham* Joan Sanderson;
Miranda Jan Francis; *Colonel Runciman* John le Mesurier; *Hopper* Roger Brierley;
Major Daintry Allan Cuthbertson; *Captain Meredith* David Griffin;
Captain Morrison Charles McKeown; *Captain Cooper* David Warwick;
The Gamekeeper Michael Stainton; *1st Mutinous Officer* Ken Shorter;
2nd Mutinous Officer Douglas Hinton; *Housemaid* Dorothy Frere;
Stunts Stuart Fell, Roberta Gibbs
Filmed on location at High Halden and Godington Park in Kent

First published in 1980 by Eyre Methuen Ltd, 11 New Fetter Lane, London EC4P 4EE
© Michael Palin and Terry Jones 1980
Reprinted 1981; first paperback edition 1981, reprinted 1981
Reprinted by Methuen London Ltd 1982
ISBN 0 413 47520 4 (hardback) 0 413 47530 1 (paperback)
Typeset by Tek-Art. Printed in Great Britain by Hazell Watson & Viney Ltd

To Alan Bell, Jim Franklin and Sidney Lotterby
and everyone who made more Ripping Yarns possible

Introduction by 'A. Viewer*'

Hello. Unfortunately I missed the first of the three new Ripping Yarns, but I caught most of the last five minutes of the second one when the tuning knob on my old Murphy stuck on BBC-2. But the third I saw from beginning to end apart from a phone call in the middle from old Archie MacIntyre in New Zealand who I hadn't seen for absolutely ages. Turned out that a huge bottle had fallen on his head in the night and he'd become a missionary. Amazing — didn't remember a thing. One moment a ventilation consultant in the Midlands, the next beloved by thousands in a small Fijian township. He, too, had missed most of the Ripping Yarns but some of his wives had seen them whilst at a 'Polygamy Now!' conference in London.

Anyway, I'm honoured to write this foreword and would have quite probably done so even if I hadn't been paid. (Every little bit helps, though, when you're as retired as I am.)

* 'A Viewer' is the pen name of Sir Humphrey de Vere Oldcastle Bart., author of the very popular 'By Camel' series: *By Camel Through Solihull, By Camel from Solihull to Wednesbury, By Camel to Castle Donnington via Beverley, Camels and the Law, Camels — Lunchtime Snack or Lifelong Friend?.* He also writes under the pseudonym 'Graham Greene'.

WHINFREY'S
LAST CASE

*A Ripping Tale of Events
That Slightly Changed the Course of History*

WHINFREY'S LAST CASE

An elegant London square. Time: the Present

A VERY FAMOUS PERSONALITY contemplates the hustle and bustle of London, then turns impressively and talks to a camera which follows his every move.

VERY FAMOUS PERSONALITY: Good evening . . . I want to ask you, if I may tonight, to join me in an experiment. An experiment to turn back time, to suspend belief in the here and now of a busy city, and to join me in the past. . . . Come with me now. (*He starts to move leading the camera with him*) . . . to a London before two wars, when this house (*He indicates a smart London residence just as a delivery van draws up against the kerb outside the house, completely blocking the VERY FAMOUS AND CHARISMATIC PERSONALITY from view. The VERY FAMOUS PERSONALITY continues to drone on obliviously, as the van's handbrake is applied and the engine rattles noisily to a halt.*

. . . was the London home of one of the most powerful men of this century. Through this elegant doorway . . .

An anoraked and stop-watched BBC PRODUCTION ASSISTANT rushes out from behind camera and across the road to ask the van to move. She runs right across the path of an oncoming Vauxhall Viva de luxe, which skids to a halt with a screech of brakes.

VERY FAMOUS PERSONALITY: . . . came and went the greatest names of pre-war days.

The P.A. approaches the driver, a MEAT PORTER, indicates the camera and asks him to move on.

. . . Kaisers, Tsars and Cabinet Ministers stood at these very windows . . .

The MEAT PORTER looks at camera, gets down from cab, and gives a cheerful nod and a wink as he goes to the back of the van.

. . . and on that balcony you see above me stood the King of England himself.

The DRIVER of the Vauxhall has now joined the helpless P.A. The DRIVER (a traveller in underwear from the Midlands) argues with the P.A. and points out how he nearly hit her.

The MEAT PORTER appears carrying a side of pig over his shoulder.

The owner of this quietly elegant residence was the legendary Gerald Whinfrey, the man who saved governments and ended wars . . . in an era when individual bravery and courage were still valued highly . . .

A terrible skid and rending crash is heard off. The Viva de luxe jerks forward. The TRAVELLER IN UNDERWEAR looks round in horror. His car has obviously been rammed. The MEAT PORTER is now quite blatantly waving at camera.

This is where our journey back in time must begin.

There is a sound of a police siren off. Slamming of doors, the MEAT PORTER gets into his cab and then out again. He performs a little dance for the camera, winking and mugging a lot. Halfway through a neat pas-de-deux an OFFICER OF THE LAW approaches, but before he can raise a truncheon the MEAT PORTER ceases his performance and nips smartly back into the cab.

. . . Take one last lingering look at this building and imagine yourselves back in the year 1913, the year of wars and rumours of wars, the year that saw the extraordinary tale (*The lorry drives off. The VERY FAMOUS AND CHARISMATIC PERSONALITY turns, at the crescendo of his oratory, to camera.*) of Whinfrey's Last Case . . . (*He comes forward and speaks to the director.*)

How was that? That felt good.

DIRECTOR'S VOICE   (*off*): One more time love . . . not quite right . . .

The VERY FAMOUS AND CHARISMATIC PERSONALITY *tears his beard off and bites the* DIRECTOR *in the head. But we don't notice, as we're busy going back sixty-seven years.*

The War Office in Whitehall, 1913.

In a war room with maps, charts of Britain, with markers all over them etc. are GENERAL CHAPMAN, *C-in-C of the Army and* LORD RAGLAN, *Chief of the Imperial General Staff. The door opens and* ADMIRAL OF THE FLEET JEFFERSON *enters.*

RAGLAN: Ah, Jefferson, glad you could get here . . . something pretty big's come up . . . sit down.

JEFFERSON   (*sitting*): What's the problem Archie?

RAGLAN: Well . . . we think the Germans may be trying to start the war a year early . . .

JEFFERSON: God! (*He looks aghast.*)

CHAPMAN   (*equally shocked*): I thought they were the one nation we could trust.

RAGLAN: We all did, Harry.

CHAPMAN: Dammit all, it's not as if we're *short* of people to have a war against.

RAGLAN: Well, suppose this damn rumour's true! . . . are we ready to start a war now?

CHAPMAN: Well, I don't know about your boys Jefferson, but we need at *least* another six months — we're still short of heavy cannons, two-point-five mortars, trestle tables.

RAGLAN: Trestle tables?

CHAPMAN: For the catering! We've only got six. You can't expect to train a man to the peak of military achievement and then ask him to eat off his lap. I mean if you spill things on some of those uniforms . . .

RAGLAN: What about the Navy, Jefferson?

JEFFERSON: We're short on spoons, mainly.

RAGLAN: No, I meant weaponry.

JEFFERSON: Ah well, we have fifteen Dreadnoughts at sea and twelve under construction.

11

RAGLAN: And the Germans?

JEFFERSON: Oh they've got everything: spoons, forks, knives, complete condiment sets . . .

RAGLAN: Ships Jefferson! Destroyers, Dreadnoughts?

JEFFERSON: Ah . . . er . . . well, the last they told us . . . it was twelve at sea and nine under construction . . .

RAGLAN: When was that?

JEFFERSON: Well I spoke to old Tirpitz at a sherry party about a month ago.

RAGLAN: Since then?

JEFFERSON: I haven't heard anything.

RAGLAN: Well this is what worries me. Intelligence think that the Germans are up to something very underhand.

CHAPMAN: Bloody Intelligence, they never did like the Germans.

RAGLAN: I'm afraid, gentlemen, they're pretty certain that the Germans have somehow opened hostilities without letting us know.

Looks of astonishment all round.

JEFFERSON: How the hell could they . . . ?

RAGLAN: I don't know how, or where or when, but we must find out, and put a stop to it before . . . (*a sharp crump as of a distantly exploding shell*) . . . what was that?

CHAPMAN: Sorry, it was my stomach.

RAGLAN: . . . Before the whole bloody country starts to panic . . . (*He stands up very straight, and gazes heroically out towards the Houses of Parliament.*) We can save this war and it can still be a Great War, but if we should fail . . . (*He looks round significantly.*) I need hardly say gentlemen, it could jeopardize our chances of ever having a war with the Germans again . . .

This really hits home. There is a long pause whilst the full awfulness of the suggestion sinks in.

JEFFERSON: What do you propose, Archie?

RAGLAN: Gentlemen, I think we have only one option: to ask Gerald Whinfrey to intervene . . .

JEFFERSON and RAGLAN: Whinfrey! Of course.

A London Club. The next day.

RAGLAN and CHAPMAN and JEFFERSON are sitting before a blazing fire. All heads are turned to WHINFREY at the mantelpiece as he swirls his brandy round the glass, stands up and takes a final drink, setting the glass down with a sharp crack on the polished marble surface. He turns to face the others.

WHINFREY: The answer is no, gentlemen. I'm afraid I can't help you this time.
RAGLAN: Whyever not, Whinfrey?
WHINFREY: Gentlemen, in the last four months I've brought the Balkan wars to an end; I've averted a revolution in Russia — for the second year running; I've sold twenty-three submarines to the French; annexed two new colonies and organized an armed uprising in Brazil. I've been saving this country every year since 1898 and I need a holiday.

All are stunned.

RAGLAN: *A holiday? . . . for how long?*
WHINFREY: A year . . . two years . . .
CHAPMAN: But . . . the war . . .
WHINFREY *(checking his half-hunter watch)*: The war gentlemen is your affair. Now if you'll excuse me I have to see George, he's lending me some fishing tackle.
RAGLAN: George?
WHINFREY: The *Fifth* . . . you know . . . ? *(He flashes a smile at the discomfited Chief of Staff and bows briefly.)* Good day, gentlemen, and good luck with your . . . war . . .

As he turns and walks out a PORTLY MAN in an armchair in the dark recesses of the club lowers his paper and calls after him.

PORTLY MAN: Don't forget you're giving my wife brain surgery next Friday, Whinfrey.
WHINFREY: Have to be after the holiday, I'm afraid.

WHINFREY sweeps out.

PORTLY MAN: Hey . . . look! I don't want her batty over Christmas!

A train rattles through a sunlit Cornish countryside. Inside a comfortable first class compartment, WHINFREY *is the sole occupant, he stares out of the window, alone with his thoughts.*

Truth to be told, I was fed up with being a hero. Having to save the country once or twice a week meant I could get nothing done at all. Well now, at last, I was going to sit back and enjoy a life of my own. I'd taken a short let on a cottage on the Cornish coast, as far away as I could get from the power politicking, and the Machiavellian intrigues of the men in Whitehall; somewhere where I could at last enjoy the real values of English life, whilst they still existed.

A small country station. The train comes to a halt with much hissing of steam, sunlight filters through the smoke. All is rather beautiful and idyllic.

WHINFREY *opens a carriage door and takes out a couple of bags and fishing tackle. He breathes in a generous gulp of fresh Cornish air and beams around happily. He can't immediately see any railway staff, however. Then he hears a footfall. He turns sharply as a* PORTER *steps out of the shadows. It is a rather distinguished man uncomfortably dressed in a brand new porter's outfit.*

WHINFREY: Ah! Porter, this is Torpoint, isn't it?
PORTER   (*he looks oddly uncomfortable, and speaks English very correctly*): Er . . . no . . . no, not really.

14

WHINFREY: But the guard's just put me off here . . .

PORTER: Er . . . no. He must have been lying. Next stop.

WHINFREY turns in annoyance as, with a whistle, the train hisses and starts to move. WHINFREY dashes after it banging his knee on the long handles of a baggage trolley. He reaches the end of the platform and stops, breathlessly watching, as the train chugs away into the distance. He turns to remonstrate with the PORTER but finds the station platform empty. He picks up his bags and starts to walk back towards the exit. As he walks something catches his eye. He stops, walks across to the overgrown railings and, bending down, pulls some weeds away to reveal a clear, and quite recently painted railway sign which reads 'Torpoint'. He looks round. The PORTER has gone. WHINFREY looks up and down the platform. There is no sign of anyone. He struggles to the booking office . . . and peers in.

WHINFREY: Hello?

Silence.

. . . Hello!

The booking office is deserted but there is evidence of a freshly made cup of tea.

Hello?

But there is nothing save a gentle wheeze from a hissing kettle. With irritated resignation WHINFREY picks up his bags and walks out of the station.

There is nothing on the station approach, just a couple of porters' barrows and some milk churns. He looks around.

No sign of life. Then suddenly he sees movement ahead of him. In the distance the elegant figure of the PORTER scuttles off round a corner.

WHINFREY: Hey!

Angry and puzzled he looks around him and sees a pub about a hundred yards away. A couple of lights are on downstairs and it looks reassuring. A sign,

'The Queen's Head' creaks gently above the door. WHINFREY *brightens and, lugging his two heavy cases, approaches it. He pushes open the door.*

Inside the pub a fire flickers in the grate. It's all quite neat, and looks ready for people, but there is no-one there.
WHINFREY *looks around. Silence. Suddenly the voice of a little old lady is heard.*

OLD LADY   (*unseen*): Yes sir?

WHINFREY *looks around, he can't see anyone. He looks around behind him; still nothing.*

OLD LADY   (*unseen*): Can I help you sir?

He swings round to the bar, walks across to it and jumps suddenly . . . he's looking down . . . there is obviously someone very small down there.

WHINFREY: Oh . . . er . . . yes . . . hello! A pint of bitter please . . . (*With relish.*) Best Cornish Bitter!

A sound of shuffling, then a little old hand comes up and pulls the pump. Nothing more of this personage can be seen.

OLD LADY: You from Penzance?
WHINFREY: No . . . no . . . London.
OLD LADY: Where's that?
WHINFREY: What?
OLD LADY: Where's that?
WHINFREY: Well . . . er . . . it's sort of east, I suppose . . .
OLD LADY: Bodmin way?
WHINFREY: No further than that . . .
OLD LADY: Oh. Russia.
WHINFREY: No, not as far as . . . Russia.
OLD LADY: Latvia?
WHINFREY: No, not as far as Latvia . . .

OLD LADY:	Estonia?
WHINFREY	(*rather sharply*): Yes, how much is that, please?
OLD LADY	(*her hand lays the pint on the bar*): Two pence, please.
WHINFREY:	Oh thank you. (*He reaches for the money.*) Cheers! (*He drinks deeply and licks his lips with satisfaction.*) Er . . . excuse me, but is this Torpoint?
OLD LADY:	Yes . . . that's right.
WHINFREY	(*frowning to himself, briefly*): Ah . . . well I'm going to be renting a little spot called . . . er . . . (*he pulls a crumpled bit of paper out of his pocket and reads*) . . . Smuggler's Cottage.
OLD LADY:	(*aghast*): Oh . . . terrible place.
WHINFREY:	What . . . ?
OLD LADY:	Terrible place to get to . . .
WHINFREY:	Oh?
OLD LADY:	Very dangerous. There's only the village taxi . . . that dares go along that road . . .
WHINFREY:	Ah, well that doesn't worry me. When can I get a taxi?
OLD LADY:	Oh . . . about five minutes.
WHINFREY:	Ah . . . that's perfect . . .

Five minutes later. A lonely moorland road.

There is a banging and clanking and a couple of sharp back-firings. Then a 1911 model T taxi chugs round the corner, weaving dangerously close to a 250-foot cliff top.

In the car WHINFREY *is sitting in the passenger seat whilst all we can see of the driver is a pair of old lady's hands turning the wheel. It is the* OLD LADY *from the pub. She chatters on quite cheerfully despite the fact that she can see nothing of the road.*

OLD LADY: It was at Smuggler's Cottage that a young retired vicar went mad . . . chopped his wife into six hundred and eighty-two pieces.

The car lurches slightly. WHINFREY *looks out apprehensively.*

OLD LADY: Bits of her were found in people's shoes for years afterwards . . .

Suddenly the car revs frantically. WHINFREY *looks even more disconcerted and grips the side.*

OLD LADY: Be a love and press that pedal down while I change gear . . .

As WHINFREY *grapples with the pedal, the* OLD LADY *goes on cheerily.*

Twenty years after that another retired vicar bought it. He used to organize knitting circles — 'Balaclavas for the Boer War' he called it. But not one of the old ladies ever came back from one of those knitting circles. Years later they were found embedded in the . . .

The car lurches wildly. A tyre skids in the earth terrifyingly close to the edge of the cliff.

WHINFREY   (*anxiously*): I think you'd better stop . . .
OLD LADY: Don't like the gory details, eh . . . ?

With more violent revving the car frees itself and jerks forward haphazardly. The OLD LADY *continues to gossip on quite unperturbed.*

Well, a year ago a retired bishop took the cottage over. He had a huge cheese grater . . .

WHINFREY   (*finally, decisively*): This is fine honestly, drop me here!
OLD LADY: All right, sir . . .

The car comes to a halt. WHINFREY *clambers out. They're at the very edge of a windswept vertiginous cliff. He reaches for his cases, then brings out his wallet for some money.*

OLD LADY: Don't worry, dear, pay me tomorrow when I bring the milk . . .
WHINFREY: Do you do *everything* round here?
OLD LADY: Oh yes . . . there's no-one else'll do this sort of work. All the young men have gone.
WHINFREY: Into the army, I suppose . . .
OLD LADY: Yes . . . I expect so.

WHINFREY *shakes his head.*

WHINFREY: What a waste!
OLD LADY: Mind how you go now . . .

The car revs up again.

WHINFREY: And you!
OLD LADY: Oh . . . I'm all right. I know this road backwards.

She starts to go into a grinding three-point turn. WHINFREY *sets his face to the wind, and looks ahead.*

He sees a lonely little stone cottage on the edge of a headland, he smiles and is about to set off towards the goal of his journey. Suddenly he hears the roar of an over-revved engine and a series of raucous crashes and bangs. WHINFREY *spins round to see the* OLD LADY *has reversed the car over the edge of the cliff.* WHINFREY *races to the top of the cliff and looks over . . .*

WHINFREY   (*calling*): Hello? Hello?

From far below the OLD LADY'S *cheery voice floats up from the wreckage.*

OLD LADY: Don't worry dear! I'm used to it!

The sound of an engine being put into gear from far below. WHINFREY *shakes his head then turns towards the lonely cottage. Far below a huge wave crashes in a mighty column of spray against the rocks.*

Further along the cliffs WHINFREY *struggles up a steep path. He stops at a broken down overgrown old sign. It reads 'Smuggler's Cottage' and has an arrow pointing ahead, and there is the cottage a hundred yards away.*

He shivers against the cold, picks up his bags and hurries towards it. As he approaches the door of the cottage, he drops his bags, looks for his key, and is about to put it into the lock when suddenly it's opened . . . A very distinguished but sternly remote professional lady in her early forties stands there with a lamp.

LADY: Mr Whinfrey?
WHINFREY: That's right . . . yes.
LADY: Welcome to Smuggler's Cottage.
WHINFREY: Oh thank you.

He enters and finds himself in a neat, but rather poky hallway, with whitewashed walls, stairs and a passage leading to a kitchen.

WHINFREY: This is very kind.

LADY: I am your housekeeper, Mrs Otway.

WHINFREY: Well this is most kind of you to bother.

MRS OTWAY: And this is my assistant, Mrs Partington . . .

A rather short young woman in a white apron appears and curtsies. WHINFREY *reacts with some surprise.*

. . . This is Mr Carne, the head steward . . .

A tall, distinguished, most unservile man appears from the passageway. He looks distinctly uncomfortable and is not un-reminiscent of the 'Porter' at the station. He bows rather stiffly.

CARNE: Evening sir . . .

MRS OTWAY: McKendrick the butler . . .

Another more elderly man appears and bows.

Mr Rothman and Mr Vickers, assistant butlers . . .

Two rather young fit men appear, again looking ill at ease and bowing rather unnaturally.

. . . McKerras the boot boy . . .

Another young man comes out of the shadows. WHINFREY *reacts in amazement.* MRS OTWAY *carries on busily.*

Mr Ferris . . .

WHINFREY: Mr . . . Ferris . . . I didn't catch what *you* do here . . .

FERRIS (*a middle-aged man, looks distinctly unhappy*): . . . Er osteopath, sir . . .

WHINFREY: Osteopath?

MRS OTWAY (*quickly*): Ostler!

FERRIS: Ostler . . . sorry ostler . . . yes . . .

MRS OTWAY (*by way of explanation*): . . . Ostler . . . stableman, you know. He attends to the horses.

FERRIS (*unconvincingly*): That's it.

WHINFREY: Well, I certainly didn't . . .

But MRS OTWAY *hasn't finished.*

MRS OTWAY: Mr Girton, master of the bedchamber . . .

GIRTON *appears down the stairs* . . .

MRS OTWAY: Mr Campbell and Mr Rowley, bedmakers . . . (*They appear.*) . . . and Mr Vinney, under assistant bedboy. (*He joins the throng.*) Monsieur Bientôt the cook . . .

A huge burly, un-French bullet-headed swaddy appears from the kitchen passageway in chef's whites with hat, behind him are two assistants also in whites.

. . . and the kitchen boys, Mr Rolfe, and Mr Tipkin . . .

The tiny hall is now packed with servants.

WHINFREY: Look, I don't know what to say, but . . .

MRS OTWAY: Say nothing, Mr Whinfrey. It's just traditional Cornish hospitality. I'll introduce you to all the gardeners tomorrow . . .

CARNE: We want you to feel absolutely at home here at Smuggler's Cottage. It's your holiday, enjoy it as you will, but don't go in the small bedroom at the end of the passage whatever you do . . .

MRS OTWAY: *Or* the basement . . .

CARNE (*silencing* MRS OTWAY *with a look*): Ssh!

WHINFREY: The basement?

CARNE: She meant the basins, Mr Whinfrey . . . don't get in the basins. They won't stand it.

MRS OTWAY: Mr Carne, show Mr Whinfrey to the bottom of the stairs.

CARNE: Yes of course. This way, sir.

They reach the bottom of the stairs in a couple of paces, but MRS OTWAY *carries on before* WHINFREY *can say anything.*

MRS OTWAY: Mrs Partington will show you to the top of the stairs . . .

WHINFREY looks up at the poky winding stairs. There are about eight steps in all.

Mr Girton will meet you at the top and take you round the corner, then Mr Vickers will take you to the door of your bedroom, and Mr Girton will take you inside.

MRS OTWAY *leaves with a severe but comprehensive smile.*

I trust you will be comfortable . . .

WHINFREY climbs the narrow stairs and is making for his bedroom when a sombre, dark-suited manservant steps out from the shadows, with a polite formal smile: WHINFREY *jumps.*

GIRTON: My name is Girton sir, I'm in charge of the upstairs section.

He indicates the bedroom door.

WHINFREY enters the bedroom, with MR GIRTON *leading. It's a traditional small cottage bedroom, with white-washed walls and very simple furniture. As they enter the room,* MR CAMPBELL *and* MR ROWLEY *stand to attention on either side of the mantelpiece . . .*

GIRTON: Passing through the door — (*He elaborately indicates what the door is.*) here, sir, you will find on your right — the bed. You will notice that it is laid with two pillows, but a further two pillows, or one bolster are available on request.
WHINFREY: Yes — thank you!
GIRTON: Should you require the pillows to be turned at any point, Mr Rowley will oblige until a proper pillow boy arrives tomorrow . . .
WHINFREY: Thank you!

GIRTON *goes across to the window and demonstrates elaborately.*

GIRTON: The curtains can be drawn, left . . . and right and left . . . and back to —
WHINFREY (*losing patience*): Mr Girton — that's *all*, thank you!
GIRTON: Yes of course, sir.

He ushers his two assistants out briskly.

WHINFREY breathes a sigh of relief then starts again rather suddenly when he hears the door open. It's MR GIRTON *again.*

GIRTON: Will you require a call, sir?

WHINFREY: NO! No thank you!

GIRTON: Well, I'll call you anyway sir, but don't in any way feel bounden by it.

GIRTON *finally leaves.*

WHINFREY *shakes his head, and slumps on the bed. There is a twang and a yell from beneath the bed and* WHINFREY *leaps up.*

Who the hell's that?

He crouches down and looks under the bed. A thin pasty-faced spotty youth is clinging on to the underneath.

VINNEY: Vinney, sir! I'm in charge of the under-mattress area.

WHINFREY: Look, go away *please!*

VINNEY (*scrambling out*): Yes, sir . . .

WHINFREY *pushes the boy out, and leans against the door, shaking his head wearily. Then he crosses to the bed, takes one last look under it and lies down.*

So began my first night at Smuggler's Cottage. I couldn't say it was the holiday I expected, but I'm sure they were all good people trying to do their best for me, and anything was preferable to the company of the warmongers of Whitehall. As I sat and listened to the silence of the night, there was something unutterably satisfying about not having to be anyone's hero . . .

The next morning. WHINFREY'S *cottage bedroom. Sun fills the room.* WHINFREY *opens his eyes, registers where he is. On holiday at last. He smiles for a moment, then a frown of concentration replaces the smile. He listens.*

In the distance, amidst the birdsong and the crashing of the sea on the cliffs below, he hears another sound. It's the sound of men being drilled, as if on an army parade ground. He pulls himself out of bed. Still listening. The noise is still there. He goes across to the window and pulls back the curtain. His eyes widen. He pushes the curtains right back and tries to pull up the window.

24

It won't move easily. As he gives it a tug a voice close behind him causes him to start. It's GIRTON, *amiably charming as ever.*

GIRTON: They're the new gardeners, sir . . .
WHINFREY: But there must be seventy or eighty of them . . .
GIRTON: Lot to do in the garden this time of year, sir: planting, weeding, cutting off the dead heads, breakfast?
WHINFREY (*looks down at the gardeners, then back to* GIRTON): What's going on here, Mr Girton?
GIRTON: Going on, sir?
WHINFREY: All these people . . .
GIRTON: They're all villagers, sir . . . We're just a normal happy Cornish fishing community.
WHINFREY: I never saw any fishermen.
GIRTON: Oh . . . they're always to be found, sir . . . In the pub usually . . . (*He laughs in a slightly forced way.*)
WHINFREY: There was no one in the pub at all yesterday.
GIRTON: Ah no . . . they weren't here yesterday . . . they were out all day . . . on the mackerel boats, sir . . . They'll be there today, though definitely. (*He turns to go.*) I'll put your kippers on, sir.

WHINFREY *turns to start dressing. He goes to the chair where his clothes were and stops in consternation. They're gone. His consternation is replaced by irritation. He marches, with brisk determination out onto the landing . . .*
He bends low along the little passage but is stopped in his tracks at the top of the stairs by the sound of MRS OTWAY *and* GIRTON *having a sharp exchange at the bottom of the stairs.*

MRS OTWAY: He mustn't leave here! D'you understand! It's as simple as that.
GIRTON (*who is holding* WHINFREY's *clothes*): I've removed his things.
MRS OTWAY: D'you honestly think that'll stop him?
GIRTON: He'll look very silly.
MRS OTWAY: Look, you're supposed to be an assistant butler, just make sure he doesn't leave the house . . . drug his kippers or something.
GIRTON: I don't think you *can* drug kippers . . .
MRS OTWAY (*impatiently*): Well just use your intelligence.

WHINFREY *darts back into his bedroom and pretends to be arranging his cravat in front of the mirror, when he hears* GIRTON's *footsteps in the passage. There is a knock on the door and a rather tentative voice.*

GIRTON: Mr Whinfrey, sir . . .
WHINFREY: Come in.

GIRTON *enters and comes up to* WHINFREY.

GIRTON: Er . . . I've just come to say, sir . . . that I forgot something earlier on.
WHINFREY (*a little cautiously*): Oh yes . . . ? What was that?

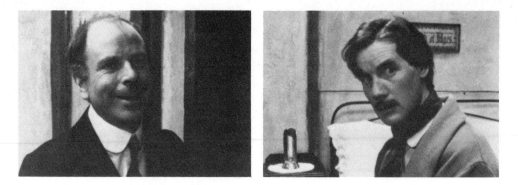

GIRTON *brings his knee up rather smartly into* WHINFREY's *groin.* WHINFREY *collapses on the floor.*

GIRTON: I do apologize, sir. But it's an old Cornish custom.

He leaves, as WHINFREY *makes to get up after him. There is a click, and the door locks.* WHINFREY *looks towards the door with grim determination.*

Whatever was going on, it certainly wasn't my idea of the ideal holiday. I decided it was probably best to forgo the kippers.

He pulls himself up and paces the room. He tries the window. It's stuck fast. He tries the door. It's solid and well-locked. Then quite suddenly his legendary cool deserts him. He races round the room in a burst of hysterical panic, trying every exit unsuccessfully. He finally pulls himself together.

However, a brief inspection of the room was more than enough to convince me there was absolutely no way I could escape. The door was oak and triple locked, the window well guarded, and there was no other entrance or exit.

He sits on the bed in despair and throws a paperweight hard at the wall in frustration. It hits the wall and falls.

But I had forgotten one thing . . . This was smuggling country.

After a series of multiple clicks, a door panel in the wall mysteriously swings open. With an expression of amazement, WHINFREY *rises to his feet and walks cautiously towards the hole. As he does so there is suddenly a click underneath him and he jumps to one side as a section of floor swings open to reveal a second set of stairs going down.*

. . . No smuggler's cottage would be complete without at least one secret passage and this seemed to be no exception . . .

He backs against a bedside table which turns over to reveal yet another set of stairs leading into a second wall: Spinning round, he almost goes down the trap door, and saves himself by grabbing a bell-pull whereupon a sky-light unexpectedly opens up in the roof and a rope-ladder dangles down. He leans back on the bed in bewilderment. It slides back into the wall, revealing a cave beneath.

In fact I discovered no less than twenty-three different secret passageways leading out of my room alone.

He finds another in the cupboard under the washbasin, two more in the floor and one in another wall.

The only problem was which one to take and where did they all lead?

WHINFREY is dithering looking at first one and then the other, trying to decide which one to take when suddenly he hears voices outside the door. He freezes. Outside are MRS OTWAY and GIRTON.

MRS OTWAY: We *have* to kill him, Mr Girton.
GIRTON: But it's against all the laws of hospitality.
MRS OTWAY: He knows far too much already . . . Out of the way.

More bolts are slid back, WHINFREY looks round panic-stricken. He makes his decision and disappears into a secret hole. There follows a series of bangs and crashes. He reappears clutching an armful of brooms and cleaning things.

More voices outside.

GIRTON: I can't do it.
MRS OTWAY: Oh give that to me and you can wipe up.

WHINFREY hears the last bolt on the door being slid back. He hesitates no longer and disappears down the trapdoor in the floor and closes it just as the door bursts open and MRS OTWAY rushes in with a large meat cleaver in her hands. GIRTON follows with a kipper on a plate.

WHINFREY leaps into the darkness of the secret passage.

MRS OTWAY   (*hisses to* GIRTON): Forget the kipper! Get the gun!

She charges after WHINFREY *with a look of grim determination.* GIRTON *goes off to exchange his kipper for something more deadly.*

WHINFREY *dimly gropes his way along the walls of a subterranean tunnel. He stops, lights a match and is looking around when the match burns his finger. He lets out an involuntary cry and drops the match. He hears a distant, echoing voice.*

MRS OTWAY: That way. Quick . . .

I staggered on blindly, and after what seemed like hours I saw light ahead and found myself free of the dank, brandy smelling tunnels.

WHINFREY *emerges onto a rocky beach.*

I decided to make straight for the village and seek help there.

He starts to clamber up the cliff. MRS OTWAY *and* GIRTON *appear.* GIRTON *fires. A bullet sings off the rocks.* WHINFREY *dodges further shots and scrambles to the top of the cliff . . . He looks down at* MRS OTWAY *and* GIRTON *and runs on towards the village.*

He sees the reassuring, creaking sign above 'The Queen's Head' and hurries towards it. As he approaches he slows down and hesitates for a moment.

From inside the pub comes the umistakable sound of lusty German voices singing a Bavarian marching song.

WHINFREY *reacts in some puzzlement then reaches the door and pushes it open.*

Immediately the singing stops.

WHINFREY *sees that this time the small single bar, with a cheerful fire in the grate, is reassuringly full of fishermen, in navy sweaters and high-sided boots. There is much cigarette smoke. All heads are turned to* WHINFREY, *who stands, faintly ridiculous in pyjamas, dressing gown, and cravat.*

WHINFREY   (*reassured at the sight of these trusty fisher-folk*): Evening!

There is some clearing of throats and a few rather uncomfortable guttural greetings which just about sound like 'Good Evening'.

WHINFREY *approaches the bar. No one there. He looks around again. This time one of the fishermen smiles stiffly back. Silence.*

WHINFREY: How do you do? My name's Whinfrey — Gerald Whinfrey.

WHINFREY *holds out his hand to first fisherman who looks panic-stricken. A colleague, who looks a little senior, rescues him.*

COLLEAGUE   (*in a very smooth faintly German voice*): Er . . . that's Tony.
WHINFREY: Hello, Tony.

The man nods uncomfortably. WHINFREY, *who's still not caught on, turns expansively to the other fishermen. The smooth German sees no way out apart from introducing them all.*

SMOOTH GERMAN   (*increasingly unhappily*): . . . And this is . . . Eddie . . . and er . . . Tony . . . another Tony . . . and er . . . Wolf . . . Wilf, sorry, Wilf . . . and er . . . Eddie . . . and another Eddie and next to Eddie is . . .
YOUNG GERMAN   (*proudly, but with heavy accent*): Eddie!
SMOOTH GERMAN   (*very unhappily*): Yes . . . another Eddie.
WHINFREY: My God, it's nice to be among sane people again. (*Rather odd reactions from the uncomprehending Germans.*) I know this may sound ridiculous, but I've just come from Smuggler's Cottage — where some of the staff are trying to kill me —

29

A voice at the door interrupts him. WHINFREY *freezes.*

CARNE: Not so fast, Mr Whinfrey, they won't understand you.

WHINFREY *turns to come face to face with* CARNE — *the 'Porter', the 'Head Steward', now dressed as a vicar.*

CARNE: I congratulate you on your persistence Mr Whinfrey. You survive the taxi ride and now you survive a night at Smuggler's Cottage. But then *the* Gerald Whinfrey would . . .

Impressed mutters from the German 'Fishermen' — 'Whinfrey . . . that is . . . Gerald Whinfrey!'

WHINFREY: Carne?
CARNE: (*clicking his heels and bowing*): Alfred Von Kahn, Mr Whinfrey, German Intelligence. (*Punctiliously he introduces.*) Fräulein Gerta Ottweg, my assistant (MRS OTWAY, *with cleaver, enters from the back door.*) . . . and Herr Gurtheim, head of our British Division. (GIRTON *with gun follows.*)

WHINFREY *looks around, slowly taking it in* . . .

WHINFREY: British Division?
CARNE: . . . A final beer perhaps for Mr Gerald Whinfrey?
WHINFREY: So long as the beer's not German as well . . .
CARNE: (*with a smile*): No the beer is authentic. (*To the* OLD LADY.) Lotte, ein echt Cornisches Bier für mein Freund, bitte.
OLD LADY'S VOICE: (*from behind the bar*): Jawohl! Mein Kommandant.

WHINFREY *turns sharply.*

A pause. The sound of shuffling, then a hand appears and takes a pint glass down. Pause. More shuffling. A hand comes up again on the beer pull.

WHINFREY: What's the game, Carne?
CARNE: Oh, it's not a game, Mr Whinfrey. We're trying to start a war. A war by other means, if you like. A war in which everyone gets a little territory and no-one gets hurt.
WHINFREY: Except the poor bastards who used to live here.
GIRTON: They're very happy . . .
WHINFREY: Well, where the hell are they?
MRS OTWAY: In Germany . . .
WHINFREY: You . . . 'captured' them, I suppose.
CARNE: No we offered them a two-year inclusive holiday in the Bavarian Alps. They all accepted very happily. Apart from the vicar, who chose Dortmund instead — he had a sister there.
WHINFREY: And you take their place over here?
CARNE: Absolutely. We have a highly trained force waiting to move into England. Six

	hundred vicars, a thousand shepherds . . .
GIRTON:	Two divisions of cockneys . . .
MRS OTWAY:	Forty-four judges . . . a dozen eccentrics . . . eight hundred and fifty private nannies.
WHINFREY:	And you expect to keep this a secret?
CARNE:	We have succeeded until now, Mr Whinfrey.
MRS OTWAY:	Until you came along.

She moves towards him. His eyes notice her gleaming cleaver.

CARNE: No. Let him have his drink first.

The OLD LADY slaps a beer noisily and contemptuously onto the bar.

WHINFREY looks round helplessly, then slowly picks up his beer and drinks. As he does so the tension increases.

WHINFREY sees GIRTON, CARNE. He registers MRS OTWAY still holding the meat cleaver.

He tries to drink slowly to save his life.

Out of the corner of his eye he sees the fishermen closing in.

The SMOOTH GERMAN comes close to WHINFREY.

He builds up a totally paranoid vision and quite suddenly WHINFREY snaps. He hurls his beer in the face of the nearest German, then races for the window. Hysterical panic sets in as he scrabbles with the lock. It won't move. He races back past the impressed but bewildered Germans and rattles the back door. That's locked. He stops and, aware that he's made a bit of a fool of himself, smooths his hair down, rearranges his cravat and gives up.

WHINFREY: All right, Carne . . . You win. What do you want?
CARNE: I just wanted to say . . . goodbye and thank you.

WHINFREY looks very bewildered. GIRTON comes up and grabs his hand.

GIRTON (*shaking hands*): Me too, Mr Whinfrey. I'm sorry about the little business of the knee in the groin earlier on. Wait till I get back to Germany . . . and tell my children I've met Gerald Whinfrey . . . It's a great moment. Good-bye, and good luck.

MRS OTWAY (*still holding the cleaver in one hand, shakes him by the other; she is looking at him in a totally new, adoring light*): Believe me, Mr Whinfrey, I would not have surrendered to anyone else but you. You are a brilliant man, you fooled us all.

Casting one last admiring glance at WHINFREY she also leaves.

SMOOTH GERMAN   (*deeply impressed*): Goodbye Mr Whinfrey . . . a pleasure to meet you.

He shakes his hand. WHINFREY *is utterly confused.*

From outside we hear the sound of a lorry arriving — military shouts. The fishermen leave, casting impressed and awed glances at WHINFREY. *They have their hands up.*

CARNE: Yes, you're quite a man, Whinfrey. We thought this operation was foolproof. But we reckoned without you. I salute you. It has been an honour to be caught out by you.

There is a clatter of army boots outside and a BRITISH CAPTAIN *and three other soldiers break in.*

CAPTAIN: All right! Get hold of them . . . come on you lot . . . out in the front.

Hand searching goes on. Revolvers are thrown on the floor. The fishermen are lined up against the wall.

WHINFREY: What the *hell's* going on . . . ?

CARNE *is hauled out by the scruff of his neck. As he passes* WHINFREY *he smiles . . . in admiration.*

CARNE: Superb job!

Then the familiar figure of RAGLAN *enters, beaming, with* CHAPMAN. *Before* WHINFREY *can say anything he grasps his hand.*

RAGLAN: Well done Gerald! You've saved the country again. And to think we believed all that stuff about a holiday. Damn glad I followed my instinct and had you tailed.

CHAPMAN: These chaps won't see much of the war now.

WHINFREY: But there won't be a war now I've caught them for you . . .

RAGLAN: Oh, there *will*, Gerald. And it'll be a *proper* one, thanks to you.

CHAPMAN: Not one of those mean little jobs run by Intelligence.

RAGLAN (*beaming confidentially*): We got definite dates from the Kaiser earlier today — 10 o'clock August 4th 1914, in France.

CHAPMAN: And if this one's successful, they want to do a follow up!

WHINFREY suddenly catches sight of a rifle slowly being raised by the tiny OLD LADY behind the bar and aimed at RAGLAN, though RAGLAN, with his back to it and pre-occupied with his triumph, doesn't notice.

RAGLAN: You're a genius, Whinfrey. I don't know how you do it. Have a drink.

WHINFREY (*looking at the raised gun*): Er . . . No . . . No, you two have a beer on me . . . I'm . . . I must get back to the holiday.

He turns and backs out of the pub rather quickly.

RAGLAN (*as he disappears*): Marvellous chap.

Outside the pub British troops are piling the Germans into the back of a lorry.

As WHINFREY walks away we hear a shot from the pub. WHINFREY stops briefly. He adjusts his cravat — another shot. He gives a sort of enigmatic smile, and walks away . . . away across the lonely cliff tops, as the sea crashes remorselessly below.

Other books in the 'Whinfrey' series
Whinfrey Goes South
Whinfrey Goes North
Whinfrey Goes South-South-East
Whinfrey Goes Mainly North-East, But Turns Ever So Slightly Westish At The Very End
Whinfrey Goes Across The Lawn To The Little Toolshed
Whinfrey Goes 'Ni!'
Whinfrey Goes Round The Twist (out of print)

GOLDEN
GORDON

A Ripping Soccer Tale

GOLDEN GORDON

Barnstoneworth, Yorkshire, 1935.

Barnstoneworth is a stout little Yorkshire wool town. A bit faded at the edges; and its prospects for the future don't look bright.

A football match is in progress, but by the sound of it, not going very well. Looking down on the dark streets of Barnstoneworth all that can be heard this Saturday afternoon is the occasional sound of a ball being kicked accompanied by grunts of pain from unfit men and groans of disappointment from a very small crowd.

In a quiet empty street of terraced houses leading up a hill, MRS EILEEN OTTERSHAW, *an aproned housewife, with hair in curlers and a headscarf, is beating a doormat against a wall. She looks up towards the sound of the football match, not very happily, finishes banging the mat and turns to go indoors.*

Back at the ground there is stuck on a rather dilapidated wooden door a poster, in handwriting, 'YORKSHIRE PREMIER LEAGUE, BARNSTONEWORTH V BRIGHOUSE. K.O. 3.00 SHARP'.

There is the sound of much straining as well as hoofing of the ball, accompanied by an occasional cough and clearing of the asthmatic throat.

Shouts of 'Kick it, Brighouse' are echoed by a lone desperately optimistic shout from GORDON OTTERSHAW.

GORDON: Get it away! Barnstoneworth. Get rid of it!

A wheeling tackle followed by the thud of a ball. Small smattering of applause. Deep groan of disappointment. A final whistle blows.

Back in the steep streets of downtown Barnstoneworth, EILEEN OTTERSHAW *pauses outside her little back-to-back and gives the carpet momentary relief,*

as she hears the final whistle ring out from the football ground. She listens keenly, then hears a familiar cry.

BARNSTONEWORTH SUPPORTERS (*thinly*): Rubbish! Ru — bbish!

With a weary sigh, EILEEN OTTERSHAW puts down the duster, hurries into the house and starts to clear away all pictures and ornaments in the sitting room. Most of the pictures are group photos of football teams. As she clears things away she calls out.

MRS OTTERSAW: Barnstoneworth?

A pallid thirteen-year-old emerges from the kitchen his expression lugubrious, his podgy fingers reluctantly marking the place in the Dixie Dean Football Annual.

BARNSTONEWORTH: Yes, Mum?
MRS OTTERSHAW: Pop down Crightons and get us some lard will you for tomorrow . . .
BARNSTONEWORTH (*glumly*): I'm learning the Barnstoneworth United reserve team of 1922, Mum.
MRS OTTERSHAW: Look . . . don't argue . . . do as I say . . .
BARNSTONEWORTH: But Mum . . .
MRS OTTERSHAW: What d'you want your Sunday lunch cooked in? Tea?

She hurries him out, pressing into his hand some money from a pot on the mantelpiece.

BARNSTONEWORTH: But Dad said he were going to ask me . . .
MRS OTTERSHAW (*ushering him out*): Hagerty F., Hagerty R., Tomkins, Noble, Carrick, Dobson, Crapper, Dewhurst, MacIntyre, Treadmore and Davitt . . .
BARNSTONEWORTH (*a little impressed*): . . . Thanks Mum . . .
MRS OTTERSHAW: Davitt scored twice in't last three minutes and Frank Hagerty saved a penalty.

BARNSTONEWORTH gives his Mum a quick smile and goes out through the front door. MRS OTTERSHAW takes a quick, and a little fearful look up the street and hurries back into the house.

As BARNSTONEWORTH walks out of the gate he looks up to see a man appearing from round the corner . . . it's GORDON OTTERSHAW, his Dad.

40

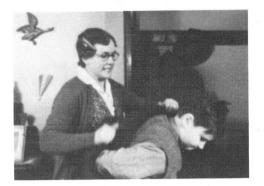

BARNSTONEWORTH   (*cheerily*): Hello Dad!

GORDON looks up momentarily, then picks up a brick off a nearby wall and flings it at his son.

Back in the house, EILEEN OTTERSHAW has quite efficiently stripped the sitting room of most of the ornaments. She stands and smoothes down her apron. The front door flies open with a crash of splintering glass. She suddenly notices she's left the clock on the mantelpiece. She makes to grab it, and is holding it when GORDON appears at the door of the sitting room. Their eyes meet for a moment.

GORDON   (*with anger dulled by years of inevitability*): Eight-one! Eight *bloody* one!

Then, quite slowly, he lifts the living room door off its hinges and smashes it to the floor. He picks up a chair and smashes it to pieces on the table, turns to the mantelpiece and finding nothing nice and breakable on top of it pulls it out from the wall bodily and hurls it across the room. He wrenches a cabinet off the wall, emptied of its normal complement of football treasures. He rips down the curtains. Then his anger still unassuaged, he leaps on the pile of rubble again, jumping up and down on it until he has no more strength. Then he turns his piteous gaze on his long suffering wife.

GORDON: Eight-one . . . To Brighouse! *Brighouse!* They're a team of old age pensioners. A tortoise with its legs tied together could dribble round that centre half. The centre-forward wears spectacles! During the game! *Eight* goals . . . four of *them* from back passes to the goalkeeper . . . oh . . . (*He holds his head.*) It was the worst . . . it was the worst . . . Oh!! (*He gives an anguished howl of pent-up anger.*)

MRS OTTERSHAW   (*softly*): I'm sorry, love.

She proffers the clock she's holding — a warm and selfless gesture. He accepts it with a weary but grateful nod and hurls it through the plate glass window into the street outside.

A few hours later, GORDON sits on the edge of a chair staring morosely ahead of him. The room looks very patched together, everything is at strange angles.

Brown gumstrip holds together the broken window glass. The curtains are torn, the tall cabinet is roped to the wall and the mantelpiece is propped in position with a couple of sticks.

MRS OTTERSHAW   (*from the kitchen*): Gordon! Yer tea's ready.

Wearily GORDON *rises and slowly, and, as if in a trance, walks through to the little kitchen. As soon as he enters* BARNSTONEWORTH *swallows a hunk of bread and dripping and proudly begins to recite.*

BARNSTONEWORTH: Yorkshire Premier League 1922 . . . er . . . Hagerty F., Hagerty R., Tomkins, Noble, Carrick, Dobson, Crapper . . . Dewhurst, MacIntyre, Treadmore, Davitt.

GORDON   (*staring, shell-shocked at the fruit-cake in the middle of the table*): Played nineteen . . . Won None, Drawn One, One abandoned due to illness, Lost seventeen . . .

BARNSTONEWORTH: Barnstoneworth United Reserve Team: Yorkshire Premier League 1922, Holton, Roberts, Carter, Sydney Cave . . . er . . . Ralph Cave, Manningham, Horsewell, Dobkins, O'Grady.

GORDON: Goals for . . . six, Goals against . . . seventy-one . . .

BARNSTONEWORTH   (*brightly*): *Junior* Team: Yorkshire Premier League 1922: Bunn, Wackett, Buzzard, Stubble, Boot, Bowman, Baxter, Broadhurst, B . . .

GORDON: Oh shut up!

He pushes his chair back and stands up.

GORDON: I'm going out.

MRS OTTERSHAW: No dripping?

GORDON: No.

MRS OTTERSHAW: (*getting up from the table and following him to the door*): . . . Gordon . . .

GORDON   (*putting his coat on*): . . . Yes . . .

MRS OTTERSHAW: Gordon . . . I've been meaning to tell you . . .

GORDON   (*abstractedly*): Mm?

MRS OTTERSHAW: I'm going to have a baby!

GORDON   (*puts his woolly supporter's hat on*): Oh right . . . don't wait up for me . . . (*He pulls open the front door.*)

MRS OTTERSHAW: Where are you going?

GORDON: Somewhere to cheer myself up . . .

A door of a nissen hut with light above it and a sign which reads BARNSTONEWORTH UNITED SOCIAL CLUB. GORDON *pushes the door open. Inside is a large empty space. An air of desolation hangs over the place. A bar at one end. A* BARMAN *stands cleaning glasses. Another man sits on a bar stool with a half-drunk pint of light and bitter, staring morosely ahead. At one of the tables sits the only other occupant of this bleak and melancholy room — another supporter staring silently into his beer.*

GORDON *walks up to the bar.*

GORDON   (*to the* BARMAN): Hello Cyril.
BARMAN: Hello . . . Gordon.
GORDON   (*nods briefly to the* MOROSE MAN AT THE BAR): Ron . . .

RON barely acknowledges the greeting.

GORDON   (*to the* BARMAN): Brown, please . . .

The BARMAN *uncaps and pours him a brown ale.* GORDON, *with a bleak smile of acknowledgement, takes it and goes to a table. He takes a sip of ale and sits broodily staring into the glass for a minute. Then quite suddenly with a bellow, like a wounded rogue-elephant, he stands up, and hurls the table onto the ground. He picks up his chair and hurls it down on top of the table. He walks across to the dartboard and wrenches it from the wall, hurling it full tilt into a table in the corner which is full of neatly laid out cups and saucers that smash noisily on the floor.*

BARMAN   (*after a respectful pause*): I know how you feel, Gordon.

GORDON turns and looks at a painted 'Honours' board which is screwed against one wall. His eye reads: BARNSTONEWORTH UNITED: YORKSHIRE PREMIER LEAGUE: RESULTS:
1925-26: DIVISION ONE: Played 40, Won 29, Drew 8, Lost 3
1928-29: DIVISION ONE: Played 40, Won 18, Drew 10, Lost 12
1930-31 DIVISION ONE: Played 38, Won 10, Drawn 6, Lost 22
1932-33: DIVISION TWO: Played 40, Won 1, Drawn 2, Lost 37
1933-34: DIVISION THREE: Played 40, Won 0, Drawn 0, Lost 40

He kicks the board savagely. It collapses and falls in two bits off the wall.

GORDON   (*with feeling*): The *useless,* useless bastards. (*He turns disconsolately for the door.*)
BARMAN: Coming to training on Tuesday night, Gordon?
GORDON   (*wearily, hand on the door*): . . . Yeah . . .

Tuesday night.

A street outside Barnstoneworth's ground. GORDON, *hands in pockets, scarf and supporter's cap on as usual, hurries along the street to the door of the ground. It's a cold day, in the greyness of an approaching evening.*

44

On the door a hastily scribbled sign reads:
BARNSTONEWORTH UNITED. TRAINING 5.30.

GORDON *pushes the rickety door open and goes in. The pitch is in reasonable condition, and there is a stand, built during more prosperous times. It now only serves to emphasize the emptiness and lack of support. A couple of supporters — the* BARMAN, CYRIL, *and another are there, blowing on their hands and stamping their feet to keep warm. A handful of players, one with no shorts on, are dragging themselves on a 'run' round the pitch. Much coughing, and stopping to spit. In the centre circle, a worried-looking man with sparse hair and the 1930's equivalent of a track suit, stands holding a ball and talking to a determined little middle-aged lady. She is* MRS ROCKWORTH, *mother of eight, one of whom is Barnstoneworth's star player. He is the Manager.*

MRS ROCKWORTH:	I'm sorry, but I'm not having our Barry come out on a night like this . . .
MANAGER:	But, Mrs Rockworth, he's our centre-forward.
MRS ROCKWORTH:	I don't care if he's Tommy Lawton. He's my son and he's not coming out on a night like this with his boils.
MANAGER:	He's a professional footballer, Mrs Rockworth.
MRS ROCKWORTH:	Is that what they call him? Six pounds a match — professional! I tell you, if it weren't for his brother being a Director of the Midland Bank and a financial adviser to the Rothschilds we'd not have two pence to rub together — so don't come 'professional footballer', wi' me!
MANAGER:	Will he be fit for Saturday . . . ? It's the Cup.
MRS ROCKWORTH:	It may be the Cup for you, it could be the coffin for him if his neck goes septic.

She turns with a flourish and marches off, she stops and turns.

MRS ROCKWORTH:	. . . Oh and Mrs Hargreaves said to tell you her Kevin's got a nasty cold sore and she's keeping him at home while Thursday . . .
MANAGER	(*bleakly*): Thank you . . .

MRS ROCKWORTH *hurries out, passing the three supporters.*

GORDON:	Good evening, Mrs Rockworth.
MRS ROCKWORTH:	Nowt good about it as far as I can see.

She goes off. In the centre circle the MANAGER *blows his whistle and summons the half-dozen wheezing wrecks who make up the backbone of his team.*

MANAGER:	Righto! Come over here, lads. I want to talk about tactics for Saturday.
FIRST PLAYER	(*plaintively*): 'E's got my shorts on . . .
MANAGER:	What?
FIRST PLAYER:	Roger Hickfield's got my shorts on . . .
SECOND PLAYER:	I have 'eck . . .
MANAGER:	Now then . . .

THIRD PLAYER: Can I go at half past six?

MANAGER: Yes . . . now then . . . Saturday as you all know is Cup-tie day . . . and it's our chance to show . . . What's the matter . . . ?

The FIRST PLAYER is sobbing.

FIRST PLAYER: He's got my shorts on, he won't give 'em back.

SECOND PLAYER: I bloody haven't . . . They were on top of my bag in't changing room.

FIRST PLAYER: They were on *my* peg.

THIRD PLAYER: They were never on his peg! I share't peg wi' 'im and I never saw 'em.

FIRST PLAYER: You're a bloody liar you are, Dobson.

THIRD PLAYER: Don't you call me names, you Pansy . . .

He hits him.

SECOND PLAYER: They were out of my bag . . .

FIRST PLAYER: They bloody weren't . . .

A punch-up starts. They all join in. The MANAGER suddenly snaps. He leaps into action, shrilling on his whistle with piercing vehemence and pulling the would-be combatants apart.

MANAGER: Stop that! D'you hear! Stop it! STOP . . . IT!

The players pull apart. The MANAGER is breathing heavily, and is clearly in a state of barely controlled nervous turmoil.

MANAGER: What the hell do you think's going on! Who the hell do you think you are! (*He glares round at the players.*) I didn't come here on a free exchange from Walsall to stand and watch a bunch of morons arguing about shorts! I came here to create a football team — a hard tough ruthless fighting unit. I don't care if your bloody shorts are on or off so long as you can do a quick one-two with an overlapping half-back . . . You can wear the sodding things over your head if it'll help you drop a long ball right at the centre-forward's feet. You can run the length of this pitch stark bollock naked if you tuck one in the corner of the net at the end of it! Shorts don't matter — d'you hear?

46

Shorts aren't what it's all about! I don't care if they're blue serge shorts, or white cotton shorts, or green flannel shorts, or sky-blue shorts with elastic-supported hand-stitched Italian-style waistbands. I don't care if they're short shorts or long shorts or three-quarter length shorts or initialled shorts or monogrammed shorts or Billy Meredith signed shorts or shorts made in Ireland or shorts made in Austria or shorts made in Timbuc-bloody-too with pink stars on that light up at night. They're *not* important! D'you hear! They're nothing to do with bloody football! The only things that matter are what's inside them . . . the machine that you've got pounding away in there. Up and down, up and down for ninety minutes.

He starts to grab and tear at the top of his shorts.

You can wear all the shorts you want . . . You can wear fifteen woolly pairs on top of each other. But it won't make a ha'porth of difference if that punching, pounding, pulsating pair inside them can't keep running and fighting and tackling . . .

He pulls his shorts down messianically.

Those are what's important. (*He slaps his marble white legs.*) Not these . . . (*He starts whirling his shorts around his head.*) Chuck 'em away! Fling 'em out . . . Forget 'em!

He races past the spectators.

Throw 'em in the bloody canal! Goodbye shorts . . . hello football!

He disappears out of the ground, buttocks glinting in the late afternoon sun. The spectators shake their heads sadly. The players stand around rather uneasily. The wind blows.

The OTTERSHAWS' *kitchen.* GORDON *tips a custard jug and spreads its contents liberally over sponge pudding.*

GORDON: . . . Indecent exposure in a bakery . . . He'll probably get three years. And that's only the manager . . . Centre forward's off wi' boils. Two half-backs are going to a wedding and the goalie's got a cold sore . . .

MRS OTTERSHAW: Gordon.

GORDON: Chairman's called an emergency meeting.

MRS OTTERSHAW: Gordon?

BARNSTONEWORTH: Dad, when were Barnstoneworth made full members of the Yorkshire Premier League?

GORDON: — 1907, Division two. *He'll* sort the whole bloody thing out . . .

MRS OTTERSHAW: Gordon, I'm going to have a baby.

GORDON: About bloody time, that's all I can say.

He stands up. MRS OTTERSHAW *isn't quite sure how to take this last remark, but at least it's better than no reaction at all.*

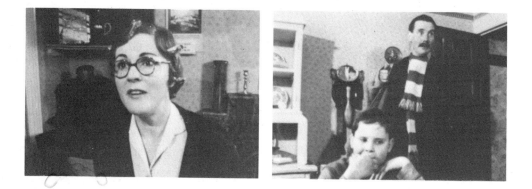

MRS OTTERSHAW: You what, love . . . ?

GORDON (*pulling his coat on*): It's about bloody time the Chairman got up off his arse and took an interest in't club. (*He puts his coat on and goes for the door.*) . . . Don't wait up for me . . . (*He leaves.*)

At the social club. The room has been heavily repaired since Gordon wrecked it. There are about ten people in the room. A table is laid up at the front, at which three notable Barnstoneworth citizens are sitting, watching people coming in. GORDON *enters and moves to a seat at the back.*

GORDON (*to the man he's sitting next to: — it's* CYRIL, *the barman*): 'Allo, Cyril.

CYRIL: Hello, Gordon.

GORDON: What's up 'ere then?

CYRIL: I think we're going to buy Arsenal's manager . . .

GORDON (*laughs briefly*): We need Arsenal's team an' all. How's Vera?

CYRIL: Not bad. Farting's stopped.

The CHAIRMAN, a short, balding, prosperous-looking little man bangs on the table for silence. He stands up and clears his throat self-importantly.

CHAIRMAN: Gentlemen and fellow supporters. The last few years have not been kind to Barnstoneworth United. One look at the Results Board will tell you that . . .

Quick cut away to the results board. It's split in two halves, which have been roughly nailed back on the wall. One half, however, has been nailed upside down.

. . . Er, this continued lack of success and consequent damage to the financial situation of this club, coupled with the loss of our manager, Mr Dainty, has impressed upon your Board of Directors the need for urgent action.

GORDON (*and others*): Hear! Hear! 'Bout time! . . .

CHAIRMAN: We have therefore decided, as from Tuesday next week, to sell Barnstoneworth United Football Club, its players, premises and ground to the Arthur Foggen Scrap Corporation for redevelopment . . .

GORDON's *face freezes.*

. . . They have assured us that the name of Barnstoneworth United will not be forgotten and have kindly consented to name one of their steel scrap crushing mills after the club . . .

Some time later. The lonely figure of GORDON standing beside the pitch at evening. His eyes are watery as he looks out of the empty stand, the CHAIRMAN's last words echoing in his head.

CHAIRMAN'S VOICE: Saturday's cup-tie against Denley Moor Academicals will be the last game at the Sewage Works ground. Believe me, we have not taken such a decision lightly — mindful as we all are of the fine traditions of our Club. But with attendance dropping consistently below the eighteen mark, with only six goals in three years, and bearing in mind the very generous financial terms offered by Mr Foggen, we feel that we have no option but to accept the redevelopment as an inevitable result of economic forces in a modern industrial society.

GORDON *wanders slowly, with utter dejection down the hill towards his house. He turns into the gate (see* GREAT MAGIC TRICKS OF HISTORY *by U. Geller, unbent editions, £5 — slightly bent, £20), and pushes the front door open.*

He enters the kitchen as if in a trance. He picks up a note on the table and reads:

'Your supper is in the oven. P.S. I am going to have a baby.'

GORDON *stands a moment then with a rumble of rage picks up the kitchen table and is about to hurl it at the wall when he stops in his tracks. Ahead of him is a day-by-day calendar. It's called 'Beautiful Barnstoneworth 1935'. It shows a suitably attractive little scene and underneath the words: 'Foggen Scrap Corporation . . . Barnstoneworth's Premier Company'.*

He slowly lowers the table, an idea is dawning. He looks at the clock. It's ten o'clock. He looks back at the calendar . . .

GORDON *appears to make up his mind . . . he turns and hurries out of the kitchen. The front door slams . . .*

In the kitchen, smoke comes from behind the closed oven door. Upstairs EILEEN OTTERSHAW, *her look of hopeful anticipation shattered again by the sound of the slamming door, sadly clicks the bedside light off.*

GORDON *cycles, suddenly hopeful, through the silent, rain-glistening street, out of the town to the gates of a very big smart house, with wide driveway. He goes boldly to the front door. He is about to ring the bell, but his determination suddenly fails him. He stops, indecisively, before the massive front door, then looks to one side, and catches sight of a sign:*

'Tradesmen's Entrance'

He turns and makes for the tradesmen's entrance. He stops again and with renewed determination retraces his steps up to the front door.

He rings the bell.

He pauses and rubs his shoes on the back of his trouser legs. He notices he has his supporter's club scarf and hat on, pulls the hat off and quickly tries to take the scarf off too. This is more difficult. An outside light goes on above his head as he's scrabbling with the scarf. He reacts . . . it makes him rush even more. He pushes his scarf into his pocket. It trails out. He pushes it in, but his hat drops out. The door opens as he's bending to retrieve the hat. A portly, impressive man, with thinning, but distinguished, brilliantined hair, stands looking down on him. He blows cigar smoke out aggressively. The epitome of the self-made Yorkshire millionaire.

FOGGEN:	Foggen.
GORDON:	Could I have a word with you for a moment?
FOGGEN:	Is it about scrap?
GORDON:	Well, it's about the Football Club . . .
FOGGEN:	Then it's about scrap . . . Come in.

GORDON enters. An opulent but tastefully furnished hall makes GORDON catch his breath in admiration, until he nearly trips over a large pile of scrap. At that moment a very elegant, expensively dressed lady, with pearls and a beautiful gown on, walks into the hall, carrying a couple of heavy railway bogie wheels, which she drops on a pile.

FOGGEN:	My wife . . .
GORDON:	How d'you do?

FOGGEN's WIFE smiles graciously, a real lady.

FOGGEN   (*indicating the pile of railway wheels as he steps over them*): Just came in today, fourteen bogies from the Scottish Railway Company. That's heavy scrap, that is . . . Worth about fifteen thousand on the open market, and I can get twenty for it . . .

As they talk the sophisticated WIFE continues transferring the bogie wheels from the elegant drawing room on to the pile in the hall, with periodic clunks and bangs. GORDON's eyes keep being diverted by her activity.

FOGGEN:	Drink?
GORDON:	No thank you.
FOGGEN	(*pouring himself a scotch from a cut glass decanter*): I love scrap, Mr . . . er . . . ?
GORDON:	Ottershaw, Gordon Ottershaw.
FOGGEN:	I've always loved scrap. Ever since I was big enough to walk I've wanted to be deeply involved with it. Well now, I've got twelve heaps in four major

cities . . . and why? Because there's only one thing I love more than scrap . . .

He sees something behind a Chippendale armchair. It's an old bicycle wheel. He picks it up and throws it across the room onto a pile. It lands accurately with a crash.

. . . and that's success. I wouldn't have anything other than success. I see it, I want it, I get it. That's my motto. In fact that's one of my many mottoes. I love mottoes. I love mottoes almost as much as I love scrap. Now, what d'you want?

GORDON: Well . . . er.

FOGGEN: Come on! *I've* been blunt with you. You be blunt wi' me.

GORDON: I . . . I . . . er . . . I want Barnstoneworth United to stay as a football club.

FOGGEN   (*approvingly*): 'I want'. I like the sound of that. Why do you 'want' Barnstoneworth United to stay as a football club?

GORDON: Well . . . er . . . well, because that's . . . what it is.

FOGGEN: Wrong! Barnstoneworth United hasn't been a football club for years. It's been a rest home for the physically incompetent. I could have had cows on that pitch for the last three years. They'd have paid for themselves *and* scored more goals.

GORDON: Well . . . we've been going through a bad patch.

FOGGEN: Bad patch! You don't know what you're talking about. D'you know when they last won a game at the Sewage Works ground, well I'll . . .

GORDON   (*leaping up, eagerly*): October 7th 1931. Two-nil against Pudsey.

FOGGEN   (*momentarily thrown*): . . . Right, but . . .

GORDON: Hagerty, Noble, Ferris, Codron, Crapper, Davidson, Sullivan, O'Grady, Kemble, Hacker and Davitt. Davitt scored both goals, one in the twenty-first minute one in the twenty-eighth.

FOGGEN: Davitt! Kenny Davitt . . .

GORDON: Neville Davitt.

FOGGEN: *Neville* Davitt, that's right. He were a player. Bald, wasn't he?

GORDON nods enthusiastically.

FOGGEN: Head like stainless steel. Ball came off it like a point two two rifle bullet. (*His eyes go misty.*) Could have got two hundred quid scrap for that head.

GORDON: Once he scored from twenty-eight yards with the back of his head against Barnsley Reserves in 1922.

FOGGEN: That was a night. Cup, wasn't it?

GORDON   (*eagerly*): Yorkshire Cup. Fourth round replay. Hagerty F., Hagerty R., Tomkins, Noble, Carrick . . .

FOGGEN: Carrick! He were a player too.

GORDON: . . . Dobson, Crapper, Dewhurst, MacIntyre, Treadmore and Davitt . . . three all. Five-three after extra time. Davitt scored twice in last three minutes, and Frank Hagerty saved a penalty.

FOGGEN: Oh aye . . . (*He pulls on his cigar.*) That were a night. There must have been ten thousand folk down there . . .

GORDON: Ten thousand, one hundred and eighteen . . . they had coaches from Leeds.

FOGGEN (*reflecting nostalgically*): Coaches from Leeds . . . eh . . . coaches from Leeds . . . (*He suddenly snaps out of it.*) Still, then's then, and now's now. First rule of scrap, never get sentimental. Time is the General Manager on our board, Mr Ottershaw. It marches on relentlessly waiting for no-one, hand in hand with the scrap merchants of this land. (*He pauses a moment.*) I wonder whatever became of Neville Davitt . . . ?

GORDON: He's got a butcher's shop over in Bradley.

FOGGEN: Old Baldy! . . . running a butcher's shop . . . ?

GORDON: Ken Carrick works in a glue factory in Todmorden.

FOGGEN: Carrick? — what a bloody waste. A glue factory for a man who could crack a goalpost in two from the halfway line.

GORDON: He works in the same shed as Harry Treadmore . . .

FOGGEN: Harry Treadmore? (*His eyes light up.*) By God, they were a team in those days.

GORDON: It can be like that again Mr Foggen, if you'll give them a chance.

FOGGEN *considers. Then his distant smile of nostalgia is replaced by the calculating frown of the businessman.*

FOGGEN: What's it to you?

GORDON: Oh, I'm just a supporter . . .

FOGGEN: I didn't know there were any of *them* left.

GORDON: Oh, there's a few of us . . . We get laughed at . . . but the way I look at it . . . that's when a team needs supporters. During the hard times . . .

FOGGEN: Listen, fifteen hundredweight of cast iron couldn't support a team that's lost its last ninety-six matches . . .

GORDON: Well, I always keep hoping something'll turn up. Another Neville Davitt, another Kenny Carrick . . .

FOGGEN (*throwing his cigar butt decisively into the fireplace, and picking up a piece of scrap*): You're getting soft again, Mr Ottershaw. Those days are gone. And they'll never come back. If they did, people like me'd be out of business. Now if you don't mind . . . (*He walks towards the door, dropping the piece of scrap on a pile as he goes.*) I've got to sort out a gross of steel filings by tomorrow . . . (*He gets to the front door and pulls it open.*) . . . Nice to talk to you . . .

He holds the front door open rather finally. GORDON *emerges and puts his cap on.*

GORDON: Yes . . . er . . . (*He's almost got tears in his eyes.*) Well, Saturday'll be last game then . . .

FOGGEN: There's plenty of good games over at Leeds these days . . . you know. You ought to get a season ticket.

GORDON: Aye well . . . I'll probably give up football for a bit.

FOGGEN: Well, goodnight.

GORDON *walks slowly down the steps, suddenly* FOGGEN *calls after him.*

FOGGEN: Mr Ottershaw!

GORDON (*turns, with a sudden resurgence of hope*): Yes?

FOGGEN: Have you ever thought of a job in scrap?

GORDON'S *face falls. He turns bitterly, picks up his bicycle and pedals off into the night.*

Next morning, in the OTTERSHAWS' *kitchen.*

A hand comes in and tears off Wednesday March 7th 1935 from the Foggen Corporation's 'Beautiful Barnstoneworth' calendar revealing Thursday March 8th 1935.

GORDON *stands staring at the calendar, with scrumpled up Wednesday in his hand.*

GORDON (*blearily: he's red-eyed and clearly hasn't slept all night*): They *can* win. I know they can.

MRS OTTERSHAW *looks rather despairingly at her husband in between rushing to get her son ready for school. She's packing him sandwiches . . . whilst he's finishing his last mouthful of breakfast.*

MRS OTTERSHAW: Come on Barnstoneworth, Let's hear them again.

BARNSTONEWORTH: Er . . . Hagerty F., Hagerty R., . . . Tomkins . . .

MRS OTTERSHAW (*angrily*): No! . . . Gladstone, Rosebery, Salisbury, Balfour, Campbell-Bannerman . . .

BARNSTONEWORTH (*tentatively*): Braggit?

MRS OTTERSHAW: No! Asquith!

She shoves the sandwiches into his hand and hurries him out of the room. We hear her shouting down the hall . . .

Asquith! Asquith! ASQUITH!

The front door slams. She comes back into the kitchen. She's very angry.

Gordon! Did you hear that? That boy's got History School Certificate today and he still gets his British Prime Ministers muddled up with the Barnstoneworth reserves for 1914. You've got to stop filling his head with football. It's not healthy! And it's no bloody use!

GORDON: Well he's not going to be a Prime Minister.
MRS OTTERSHAW: And he's not going to be a footballer, is he . . . ?

This hits hard.

GORDON (*quietly*): He may be . . . yet.
MRS OTTERSHAW: You know he can't kick a ball straight. He hates it. And how would you like to be called 'Barnstoneworth'?
GORDON: He's got another name . . .
MRS OTTERSHAW: United! What sort of name's that? I wish you'd let him do what he wants, Gordon. Hagerty, F., Hagerty, R., Tomkins, Noble, Carrick, Davitt . . . It doesn't matter! When will you realize, Gordon, that it doesn't matter who the hell played for Barnstoneworth bloody United in 1922!

She stops, suddenly anxious that she's gone too far. But amazingly, as she looks, a big grin spreads across GORDON's face.

GORDON: Yes . . . oh, yes . . . (*Dawning realization.*) Of course! (*He makes for the door.*) Of course!

He turns and grins at her as he pulls his coat on. She follows him to the door.

MRS OTTERSHAW (*following*): Where are you going?
GORDON (*he picks up his bike*): Bradley!
MRS OTTERSHAW: Bradley! What for?
GORDON (*calling back*): Shopping!
MRS OTTERSHAW: Gordon, before you go *any* where, we must talk.
GORDON: Don't wait up for me love.

He cycles off.

MRS OTTERSHAW (*reacts for a moment, then yells after him*): Gordon! *I'm going to have a baby!*

A passer-by, a sallow spotty young man, looks up . . . and reacts to this with some embarrassment.

MRS OTTERSHAW with an angry little cry of frustration, slams the door.

GORDON cycles, with newly-found enthusiasm, along lanes, by dry-stone walls, and across the Yorkshire moors until he coasts down a hill and past a sign 'Bradley'.

He cycles up to a corner shop and looks up at the name with a hopeful smile . . . E. & R.J. DAVITT, HIGH CLASS BUTCHER. He parks his bike . . . pushes open the door to the butcher's shop, a man looks up from behind the counter. He has a very obvious thick head of artificial hair.

GORDON: Mr Davitt? Neville Davitt?

DAVITT looks round in rather quick, furtive alarm.

DAVITT: (*cautiously*): Yeah . . .
GORDON: Er . . . my name's Gordon Ottershaw. (*He finds himself staring at DAVITT's luxuriant hairpiece, fascinated.*) . . . er . . . I'm from Barnstoneworth.
DAVITT: (*unhelpfully*): Oh yes . . .
GORDON: Oh yes . . . I was a great fan of yours when you used to play for United . . . I remember your . . . er . . .
DAVITT: Yes?
GORDON: Your er . . . Well . . . before you . . . well when you still had er . . .
DAVITT: Fastest legs in West Yorkshire?
GORDON: Er . . . yes . . . and er . . . of course your specialities . . . you know . . . all those goals from the er . . . er . . . (*He can't stop himself looking at the elderly ex-footballer's bonce.*)

DAVITT: Penalty spot?

GORDON   (*embarrassed now*): Yes . . . yes . . . and with the er . . . well, with the headers, you know . . .

DAVITT: No. Never scored with my head. Couldn't afford to with a head of hair like this . . . I was always proud of my hair, always will be.

But GORDON perseveres with DAVITT. A few remarks are exchanged and when GORDON re-emerges, he looks encouraged and mounts his bike jauntily.

At the doorway of a factory, marked BRITISH GUM LTD. TODMORDEN WORKS *GORDON is talking to a couple of old men, both in caps. At first much shaking of the head . . . one has no teeth at all. Then one of them gives a bit of a smile, a nod . . .*

An elderly man is being pushed by a nurse along a path at an old folks' home. He coughs a little and looks around. Obviously very frustrated and bored. Suddenly he looks up . . . A figure cycles up the drive. It's GORDON. He stops, gets off his bicycle, and goes up to the man in the chair . . . He talks for a moment. The man looks puzzled. GORDON explains. The man nods eagerly, shakes his hand, and GORDON runs back to his bicycle . . .

GORDON cycles to a group of railway cottages, and shouts up. A man at an upstairs window in a dressing-gown nods at GORDON down below on his bike. They talk a while, then both nod, wave and GORDON cycles off again.

GORDON cycles off to a church in a small village. He stops his bike, gets off and walks into a graveyard. He walks amongst the mass of gravestones. Suddenly he looks ahead and down and his eyes light up. He calls down to the gravedigger in a hole. The man turns, puzzled. GORDON walks up to him, shakes his hand, the man nods . . . GORDON talks . . . and sets off again . . .

Saturday afternoon.
The main, and indeed only, gate of the Sewage Works ground. There is a bold sign on the door: YORKSHIRE CUP. BARNSTONEWORTH UNITED VERSUS DENLEY MOOR. K'O. 3.00.

A couple of people go in. A large smart Riley saloon comes to a halt outside the ground. The door opens. The CHAIRMAN gets out with his wife, in a fur, looking as though she's loathing every minute of it. He scowls as he sees the sign on the door, and walks briskly past it and into the ground.

CHAIRMAN: Bloody embarrassing this is going to be . . . Should have called the whole match off — half the team sick or missing. Why the hell we couldn't . . .

He turns and finds himself confronted by FOGGEN.

CHAIRMAN: Oh, Mr Foggen . . . haven't seen you here for a few years. Come for a look at the premises eh? Make a lovely scrapheap this will.
FOGGEN: No, I've come to see Barnstoneworth win a match.
CHAIRMAN *(laughes dismissively):* Well, I shouldn't hang around getting cold if I were you, Mr Foggen. We haven't even got a full team . . .
FOGGEN: Your Mr Ottershaw thinks they'll win . . .
CHAIRMAN: Ottershaw! Don't go worrying about him, Mr Foggen.
FOGGEN: He's enthusiastic . . . I like enthusiasm.
CHAIRMAN: Obsessed, I call it. It's a form of madness, you know . . . wearing your scarf in bed, calling your kids 'Barnstoneworth'.
FOGGEN: I'd like to see them win again, though.
CHAIRMAN: I'd like to see them turn up . . .

There is a cheer from the massed Denley Moor supporters as their team runs out.

CHAIRMAN: That's Denley Moor . . . good team. They've got young Olthwaite at number eight.
FOGGEN: Oh aye . . . the bank robber?
CHAIRMAN: It were never proved.

A few shouts from Denley Moor supporters, who wave flags and make a lot of noise.

CHAIRMAN: Oh come on Barnstoneworth, where are you?

He looks at his watch, then looks towards the pavilion. On the pitch the Denley Moor team are whistled to the centre by the REFEREE. *They turn towards the pavilion waiting.*

CHAIRMAN *(checking his watch):* Three o'clock!

He looks anxiously round for any trace of his team.

After a moment a figure emerges. It's the MANAGER, ERIC DAINTY, *in a long brown mac from which his white but knobbly legs protrude rudely. He hurries towards the* CHAIRMAN *rather pathetically.*

FOGGEN: Who the hell's that?
CHAIRMAN *(embarrassed):* . . . Our ex-Manager . . .
FOGGEN: What the *hell's* going on?

YORKSHIRE CUP

BARNSTONEWORTH
UNITED
V.
DENLEY MOOR

K.O. 3%

MANAGER: There's only four turned up sir, and only one of them's got shorts.

CHAIRMAN: I don't believe you.

MANAGER: *I could play . . . I could show them a thing or two . . .*

CHAIRMAN: Yes I'm sure you could Mr Dainty . . . but that's not what they've come to see. No, I'll go and cancel . . . What a bloody way to go . . .

He makes to walk to the REFEREE, *when suddenly he is stopped by the sound of a coach drawing up outside. The coach doors slam, then the gate to the ground flies open . . .* GORDON OTTERSHAW *comes running through.*

CHAIRMAN: Ottershaw . . .

GORDON (*holding the gate open*): Sorry we're late!

Into the ground come eleven elderly and middle-aged men in Barnstoneworth colours and long shorts led by NEVILLE DAVITT *(with his wig on), bouncing the match ball, followed by the two men from the glue factory, the gravedigger and all the others* GORDON *recruited. All heads turn as they run on to the pitch. The last of all in the team is the* OLD MAN *from the old folks' home.*

He's pushed on in a wheelchair by his same reproving nurse. She pushes him to the touch-line. He throws off the rug and reveals himself in the full splendour of the Barnstoneworth strip. He canters on to the pitch. Some startled applause. The Denley Moor team look on with amazed, somewhat disdainful smiles.

The REFEREE *whistles the captains together.* DAVITT *(60) and the young Denley Moor captain come together. They toss. After the toss the teams line up. Just as the whistle's about to go,* DAVITT *with a dramatic timing throws aside his toupee, to reveal the deadly pate, freshly greased and shining. Now there really is a reaction. Even the Denley Moor players know who it is. A rustle of excitement.*

FOGGEN's *face lights up. Then cheering breaks out . . .* GORDON *looks proud fit to burst . . .*

The whistle goes. The ball goes out from the gravedigger, to the man from old folks' home, who manages to turn past a player and fire a long pass out to the wing with amazing accuracy. The nurse winces as she watches. The ball goes to BALDY DAVITT *who swerves and twists, quite magically to the almost extinct sound of Barnstoneworth cheers.*

The CHAIRMAN *is still stunned as* DAVITT *weaves past a back and cracks in a shot and it's a goal. As the team rush up to congratulate him, the Denley Moor goalie picks himself up from the mud, goes up to a bewildered small fan who stands beside the goal, grabs his autograph book and pencil, thrusts the fan rudely to one side and rushes up to* NEVILLE DAVITT, *proffering the book.*

The REFEREE *points to the centre-spot. Cheers and applause. The Denley Moor supporters are stunned into silence.*

Ninety minutes later outside the little Ottershaw home.

MRS OTTERSHAW *is beating the doormat again when she hears the whistle go. Instinctively she makes to go in to protect her home, when suddenly she freezes.* BARNSTONEWORTH, *her son, appears silently behind her, and he too gazes up the road in disbelief, for what they can hear is cheers, not groans.*

SUPPORTERS: Barnstoneworth! Barnstoneworth!

As the cheers die away, the sound of running feet getting nearer. Round the

corner of the top of the hill comes GORDON. *He races down the road . . .*

MRS OTTERSHAW *ushers her son into the sitting-room. She's a bit worried by this unexpected turn of events.* GORDON *crashes into the house and flings the sitting-room door open. His face is hot, radiant and suffused with joy!*

GORDON: Eight-one! Eight . . . Bloody . . . One!

A slight pause, then all three of them as sheer delight dawns on their faces, turn and start to smash the sitting-room up. With joyous abandon they take the little place apart. Celebrating in an orgy of destruction the almost unbelievable fact that Barnstoneworth United have won a match. At last the OTTERSHAW *family are truly happy.*

*The Ripping Tale of a Young Man
caught in a World of Changing Values
and forced by Circumstances to the
Most Despicable Act known to the British Army*

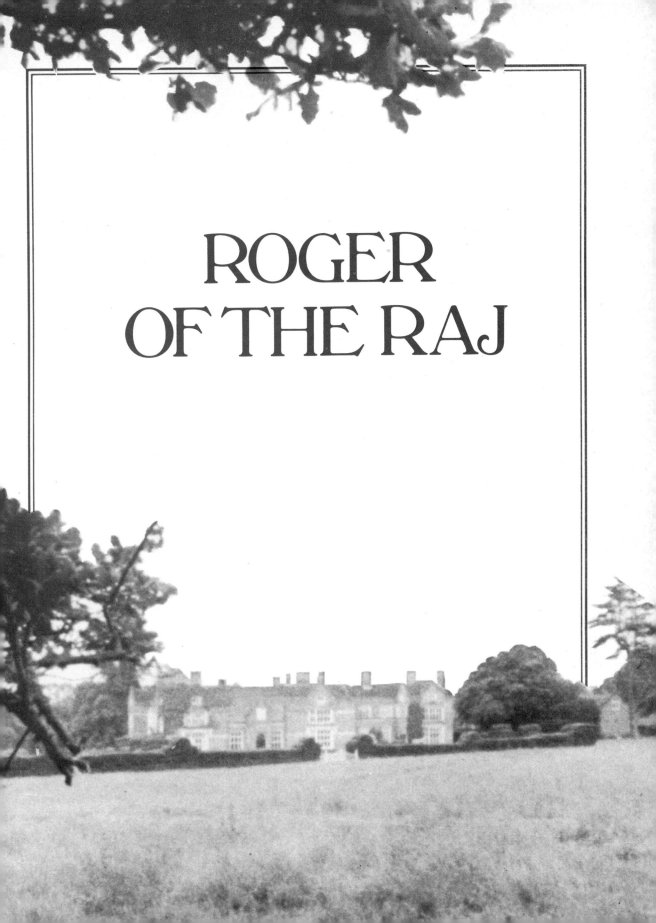

ROGER
OF THE RAJ

India

ROGER OF THE RAJ

England 1914

*Deep in the heart of the English countryside stands the stately edifice of
Bartlesham Hall — home of the Bartlesham family for six proud generations
(or probably less). This is the story of the son and heir to the Bartlesham
estate, Roger Bartlesham, and how he stooped to the most despicable
act known to the British army. It is he who now takes up the tale.*

The reasons for what I did in India that fateful night in 1917 really began
in my childhood . . . I was luckier than most boys of my age in that my
father did have enormously large amounts of money, enabling us to be
mercifully free of the everyday anxieties of life — such as lack of houses
and tennis courts. The endless leisured days at Bartlesham Hall began, as
always, with the family breakfast.

A typical family breakfast finds ROGER *marooned in the middle of a
lengthy refectory table, with his mother,* LADY BARTLESHAM, *at one end
and his father,* LORD BARTLESHAM, *at the other.*

*On a sideboard behind him stretches the vast profusion necessary to
sustain life at Bartlesham Hall during the long hours before lunch. There
are devilled kidneys, eggs and bacon, scrambled eggs, kedgeree, sausages,
scotch woodcock, steaks, toast, halibut, kippers and little pastry brioches,
all lavishly laid out in silver serving dishes, heated by spirit lamps. Bread
and butter, a tea canteen and numerous coffee pots also stand at the
ready. On another, even larger, sideboard silver salvers groan with a choice
of cold meats — pressed beef, ham, tongue, pheasant, grouse, partridge,
ptarmigan. There is also a side table, heaped with fruits — melons, peaches,
raspberries, nectarines.*

LORD BARTLESHAM *is quite elderly, and is reading a paper as is clearly his
wont. He is an amiable man, with a vaguely distant, reflective air.* LADY
BARTLESHAM *is a dominating tight-lipped, rather severe lady. She sits bolt
upright, eating toast with a sharp staccato crackle. This is the only sound*

67

in the room, apart from the deep tick of a clock . . . until LADY BARTLESHAM *finally breaks the silence.*

LADY BARTLESHAM: The toast is frightfully good today, Barty.
LORD BARTLESHAM: Yes . . . yes . . . it was awfully good.
LADY BARTLESHAM: Very pleasantly brittle.
LORD BARTLESHAM: Yes . . . really very good toast.
LADY BARTLESHAM (*after a short pause*): I think it's some of the best toast we've ever had.
LORD BARTLESHAM: Yes . . . yes . . . could be . . .
LADY BARTLESHAM: I wonder who made the toast today?
LORD BARTLESHAM: Well . . . whoever it was — they're a dab hand.
LADY BARTLESHAM: Mrs Angel?

The HOUSEMAID *turns from the sideboard.*

Who made the toast today?

MRS ANGEL: Er . . . Judy, I think, your Ladyship.
LADY BARTLESHAM: Well, commend her most highly.
MRS ANGEL: Yes, your ladyship . . .

She curtseys and withdraws.

As she passes LORD BARTLESHAM *he looks up from his paper.*

LORD BARTLESHAM: Set her free, Mrs Angel . . .
LADY BARTLESHAM (*exchanging a brief glance with* MRS ANGEL): She *is* free, dear.

MRS ANGEL *leaves.*

LORD BARTLESHAM: Judy . . . free? Surely not.
LADY BARTLESHAM: They're all free, dear . . . all the servants. There's been no slavery in this country for donkey's years.
LORD BARTLESHAM: But Judy — little slip of a girl, washes floors all day long . . .
LADY BARTLESHAM (*a hint of impatience*): She's still free, dear . . .
LORD BARTLESHAM: Well, I think it's a great shame . . .

LADY BARTLESHAM: *What* is a shame, dear?

LORD BARTLESHAM: Not being able to free people. (*He lays his paper down and his eyes begin to glisten.*) It must have been a wonderful thing to do . . . just sort of free a chap . . . some poor miserable wretch in chains . . . and along you come and say . . . 'You're free! You're a free man . . . Off you go! Run around wherever you want!' Imagine the new life that's about to open up for him.

LADY BARTLESHAM: Not in front of the boy, Barty.

LORD BARTLESHAM: (*as if awaking from a reverie*): What?

LADY BARTLESHAM: You're not to become emotional in front of the boy.

LORD BARTLESHAM: Sorry.

LADY BARTLESHAM: And what are you going to do today, Roger?

The boy is taken off guard.

ROGER: Oh . . . er . . .

I dreaded these moments, when mother would suddenly talk to me. Fortunately, they were mercifully few, but I never seemed to have an answer ready.

ROGER: I . . . shall be doing some Latin translation with Mr Hopper.

LORD BARTLESHAM: Hopper? He's a child-molester, isn't he?

LADY BARTLESHAM: He *was* dear. He is no longer.

LORD BARTLESHAM: Are you sure?

LADY BARTLESHAM: Yes, dear.

She cracks some toast rather conclusively.

Another part of the house. Some time later.
ROGER is sitting with an open exercise book and pencil ready.

A youngish man, gaunt and rather good-looking in a dark, wild-eyed way and in a well-worn suit, turns from a bookshelf and strides across the room, gesticulating, rather dramatically.

Mr Hopper knew no Latin at all. In fact his only qualification as my tutor was a forged degree from the Department of Botany at Bangkok University. Instead, he used to teach me social revolution.

From ten in the morning until six in the evening, he told me all there was to know about Socialism, Marxism, the State Ownership of Capital and the bloodshed that would inevitably follow the armed uprising of the proletariat.

A shotgun shatters the quiet.

The shotgun is held by LADY BARTLESHAM. *She,* LORD BARTLESHAM, ROGER *and* MR HOPPER *are on the grouse moor, concealed behind a magnificently constructed hide.* LADY BARTLESHAM, *however, is the only one doing any firing. She is wreathed in smoke and firing off volley after volley of shot, whilst a gamekeeper supplies her with freshly-loaded shotguns from a large pile.*

LADY BARTLESHAM:	Come on, Roger. (*Bang.*) Shoot away!

ROGER *looks fed up, but nevertheless fires.*

LADY BARTLESHAM	(*Bang*): And another! (*Bang.*) And another! There we go! (*She turns to* LORD BARTLESHAM.) Come on, Barty, kill something.
LORD BARTLESHAM:	Oh sorry dear. (*He, too, fires, but without tremendous enthusiasm.*)
LADY BARTLESHAM:	Come on, Hopper! (*Bang.*)

My mother had killed more grouse than any other woman in history.

LADY BARTLESHAM:	There's a nice fat one! (*Bang.*)
GAMEKEEPER	(*handing her another gun*): That's Mr Barlow, ma'am.
LADY BARTLESHAM	(*peering rather crossly out of the hide*): So it is. Oh drat! Barty, we must *not* choose beaters that look like grouse. I've just shot Barlow.
ROGER	(*in some alarm*): I'll go and get him!

LADY BARTLESHAM *fires another volley, whilst* MR HOPPER *restrains* ROGER.

HOPPER:	Ssh!
GAMEKEEPER	(*helpfully*): He's been shot before, ma'am. I'm sure he won't mind.
LADY BARTLESHAM:	It's just such a waste of cartridges!

Bang.

LORD BARTLESHAM	(*to* HOPPER): Jolly decent sort of chap you know . . . the average slave.
LADY BARTLESHAM	(*automatically*): Servant, dear.

Bang.

ROGER:	Are you just going to *leave* him there?

LORD BARTLESHAM:	Well all right, 'servant' if you like . . . (*Aside to* HOPPER.) I don't know what's wrong with a good old-fashioned word, sometimes.
HOPPER	(*smiles*): Well yes, sir, I often find modern jargon offensive. (*He lays a resting hand on* ROGER, *calming his indignation.*) Sssh!
LADY BARTLESHAM	(*Bang*): It's inaccurate, that's what's wrong, dear. (*Bang.*) Barlow is a servant. He's a free man. Isn't that right Kenton?
GAMEKEEPER	(*touching his forelock*): Yes, ma'am.
LADY BARTLESHAM	(*Bang.*)
LORD BARTLESHAM:	Well, wonderful chap, anyway.
LADY BARTLESHAM	(*Bang bang.*)
LORD BARTLESHAM	(*starting to go into a reverie again*): Being free and yet willing to be constantly shot.
ROGER:	I don't think he *wants* to be shot, Father. I don't think anyone *wants* to be shot in the back.
LADY BARTLESHAM	(*overhearing*): You'd be surprised . . .some of these people quite like it (*Bang.*) . . . gives them a certain security (*Bang.*) . . . not everyone can cope with success and good health all the time. Isn't that right, Mr Hopper? (*Bang.*)
HOPPER:	Oh yes, there's a lot in that, your ladyship.
LORD BARTLESHAM:	Well it makes me feel humble . . .
LADY BARTLESHAM	(*Bang.*)
HOPPER:	What, sir?
LORD BARTLESHAM:	Chap like Barlow — with all the world to choose from — will repeatedly lie face downwards in the field without a single word of complaint . . . God! I know of chaps who'd moan about the skin on top of their porridge — and they're rich chaps too . . . intelligent, well-educated . . . and yet there's Barlow — a simple slave — lying in the mud without the slightest murmur of animosity.
LADY BARTLESHAM:	Do stop talking, Barty, you haven't shot anything for ages . . . (*Bang.*) Fire up, Roger, come on . . .

ROGER *throws his gun down and climbs out of the hide.*

ROGER:	Shoot your own beaters!
LADY BARTLESHAM:	Roger!

ROGER *walks away.*

LADY BARTLESHAM:	What on earth's the matter with the boy . . . ? What's wrong with shooting, for heaven's sake . . . ?

In the twinkling of an eye, however, Lady Bartlesham's shotgun is replaced by the blast of cannon and the boom of heavy artillery, as mud-soaked troops race across the benighted battlefields of Belgium and France.

Besides being immensely rich, my father was also Honorary Colonel of the Dorsetshire Rifles. And in 1914 we found ourselves uprooted from Bartlesham Hall. We were sent four thousand miles away to the Punjab, to do our bit in the Great War for Civilization . . .

India 1914.

The scene changes abruptly to a gentle croquet match on the elegant lawns outside the Colonel-in-Chief's Residence in the Punjab. All the family is there, including MR HOPPER, *who now sports an unmistakably Russian hat.*

Mr Hopper was so pleased to be near Russia, he changed his name to Leon Hopper and bought a new hat.

At this moment, it becomes clear that the young ROGER's *attention is being attracted by the delicately beautiful features of a young girl who is also playing.*

LADY BARTLESHAM: Your turn, Barty.

An INDIAN SERVANT *walks up to* LORD BARTLESHAM *and takes his mallet. The* INDIAN *then proceeds to hit an extremely accurate shot which wins the game. He hands the mallet back to* LORD BARTLESHAM *and everyone applauds.*

ALL: Oh well done, sir!
ROGER: Nice shot, father!

Once again, however, the scene changes — this time to an elaborate dinner amidst the candle-lit splendour of the Colonel-in-Chief's dining-room. The officers are all resplendent in their elegant dress uniform, and the ladies look beautiful.

The evenings were taken up with endless regimental dinners . . . the same people . . . the same talk . . . until one memorable night, as the women were retiring . . .

LADY BARTLESHAM: Well, shall we retire, ladies?

The ladies rise. Pleasant smiles are exchanged all round, as LADY BARTLESHAM *indicates the withdrawing room.*

CAPTAIN MORRISON, *a rather dashing young buck, leans expansively back into his chair, glass of wine in hand.*

CAPTAIN MORRISON: We'll be in to spank you later — you firm-buttocked young Amazons!

The whole room freezes. A ghastly silence falls.

CAPTAIN MORRISON (*rising, ashen faced*): I'm terribly sorry . . . I don't know what came over me . . .

The ladies are ushered quickly out by LADY BARTLESHAM. LORD BARTLESHAM stares fixedly at the table.

LORD BARTLESHAM: That's all right, Morrison. I think you know what to do.
CAPTAIN MORRISON: Yes, yes . . . of course, sir.

MORRISON walks to the door. He turns.

CAPTAIN MORRISON: I apologize to you all.

He leaves, closing the door behind him. There is a brief pause, followed by a gunshot and the thud of a falling body. At this the silence is broken. Everyone loosens up, the conversation starts to flow again, and the port is passed around.

RUNCIMAN: Pity really, he was a nice enough chap . . .
DAINTRY: Yes . . . talented, too. He could have been number two in the War Office if he'd lived.
MEREDITH: Friend of yours, wasn't he, Clive?
COOPER: Yes . . . he was my best friend in the Regiment.

Meanwhile, at the other end of the table LORD BARTLESHAM is talking to RUNCIMAN, his second-in-command.

LORD BARTLESHAM: I can't understand what makes a man ruin a career like that.

There is general agreement at this, and then everyone lapses into table talk once more. COOPER, however, suddenly turns to MEREDITH, on his right, and pushes the port towards him.

74

MEREDITH:	Hey, Clive, what are you doing?
COOPER:	Don't you want any port?
MEREDITH	(*with a quick, alarmed glance at the others*): Dammit, Clive . . . don't be a fool.
COOPER:	I thought you liked port.
MEREDITH	(*as if the joke's gone far enough*): Not like *that* . . . come *on! Right* to *left!*
COOPER:	Let's pass it the other way for once.
MEREDITH	(*in genuine alarm*): Clive, don't be a bloody fool! Think of your wife and children and the Regiment . . .
COOPER:	(*recklessly pressing the port on the reluctant* MEREDITH): Come on! Take it!

MEREDITH shies back. LORD BARTLESHAM *notices for the first time.*

LORD BARTLESHAM:	I say, Cooper! What's going on?
MEREDITH	(*covering up*): It's nothing, sir . . . he was just asking me . . .
COOPER:	I was passing the port from left to right.

There is a stunned silence. All heads turn to COOPER, *who looks defiant.*

LORD BARTLESHAM:	Off you go, Cooper.

Everyone looks down at their plates as if avoiding seeing COOPER. *You can cut the atmosphere with a butter-knife, as* COOPER *rises.*

COOPER:	All right! I'll go! But I want you to know that I don't care . . . d'you hear me . . . I don't care . . . If that's the way you want to pass the port — you pass it. But you can pass it without me.

He turns and stalks out slamming the door behind him. There is a pause. Then a shot.

LORD BARTLESHAM:	Well perhaps we can carry on . . . cigar, Runciman?

MEREDITH *pushes his chair back and stands up.*

MEREDITH:	I want to go too! I think it's about time someone said what Cooper has

just said! I think *anyone* should be allowed to pass the port any way they want . . .

LORD BARTLESHAM (*sympathetically, but anxiously*): Meredith!

MEREDITH: Left to right! Right to left! Diagonally!

LORD BARTLESHAM (*more sharply*): Meredith!

MEREDITH: Under the table! Over the table! Behind one man, in front of the next . . . one-handed, two-handed . . . first one way, then the other.

LORD BARTLESHAM: Meredith!

MEREDITH (*in full swing*): Two to the left and three to the right! Missing every third person on one side! Every alternate person on the other!

LORD BARTLESHAM (*as commandingly and definitively as possible*): MEREDITH!

MEREDITH stops. He tosses his head back and looks at them defiantly.

Then he too, rises and leaves. The door shuts. There is a pause. A gunshot.

Everyone relaxes and the conversation starts up again amongst those who are left. But more is to come . . . DAINTRY gets up . . . fiery-eyed.

DAINTRY: May I say it's more than just *passing* the port that's at stake here? I believe . . . that the *women* should be allowed port as well . . .

Gasps of disbelief from all. This really is heresy.

LORD BARTLESHAM (*more in kindness than in anger*): Daintry, sit down . . . (*To RUNCIMAN.*) It must be the heat . . .

DAINTRY: No no! I want to speak! I feel that women should be allowed to drink port *and* brandy *and* madeira!

LORD BARTLESHAM: *Daintry!* You're overtired!

DAINTRY: And they should be allowed to sing! And dance! And throw their heads back in laughter, and toss their beautiful hair! And smile and make the world a finer, happier, saner place!

LORD BARTLESHAM (*with weary resignation*): Off you go . . .

DAINTRY walks out. There is a shot and the sound of breaking china from the hallway, and DAINTRY's voice drifts back.

DAINTRY: Damn.

There is another shot followed by a satisfied grunt, and the thud of a body hitting the floor.

LORD BARTLESHAM and RUNCIMAN (an older, more distinguished and experienced officer) are left alone at the end of the table.

LORD BARTLESHAM takes a sip of port and shakes his head sadly.

LORD BARTLESHAM: Such a damn fine soldier, Daintry . . . don't you agree?

RUNCIMAN	Yes! Damn fine, Barty, damn fine . . . and honest. (*He stands.*) I've wanted women in here for years.
LORD BARTLESHAM:	What?
RUNCIMAN:	Yes, *I've* wanted to pass the port from left to right just as young Daintry did . . . but more than that! (*Pause.*) I've wanted to do away with the Loyal Toast!
LORD BARTLESHAM:	Oh no! Runciman! Not you. (*He shakes his head in disbelief.*)
RUNCIMAN:	I've wanted to abolish the National Anthem! I've wanted to set up a Socialist Republic in this land . . . a state where those who *do* the work shall be given the full reward of that work . . . where privilege and patronage shall be cast away and one man shall be equal with his fellow! *Smash* the Monarchy! . . . *Smash* the Ruling Classes! *Break up* the homes of the Rich and Privileged and let all humanity share equally, as God surely intended them to do!

He marches proudly out. There is another shot and the sound of a body smartly hitting the floor.

LORD BARTLESHAM *hangs his head wearily, sitting in pathetic isolation at the head of the table.*

Suddenly, as if for the first time in his life, he looks up and notices his son, sitting silently, head hung in embarrassment at the end of the table.

Mr Hopper had once told me that a moment like this would come, when the old order would finally collapse, and I was to let him know if it happened while he was out.

Suddenly ROGER *stands up, hurls his glass into the fireplace and stalks out.*

But I had plans of my own.

ROGER *marches down the corridor and out of a side door, and runs towards the servants' quarters.*

Finally he arrives in the main larder. He runs his eye around the fine stock

of pheasant, grouse, duck, chicken, beef and pork, selects the two largest legs of lamb and makes off, out of the house and down the drive. He has almost reached the end of the drive when a guard dog leaps out at him, barking fiercely. ROGER throws one of the legs of lamb to the dog, who immediately stops barking and gratefully sets to ripping it apart.

ROGER runs on, unharmed, through the gates and down the road. Turning in at the drive to the next big house, he is once again faced by a fearsome guard dog. He throws the second leg of lamb for it, and then continues up to the house. Scaling the outside of the house with some agility, he reaches the window of Miranda's bedroom. He lets himself in to find the HONOURABLE MIRANDA at her dressing table, combing out her fine, long hair.

ROGER: Miranda!

MIRANDA: Roger! What are you doing here?

ROGER (*eyes shining eagerly*): Have you thought it over, Miranda?

MIRANDA: Yes, but my parents would never allow it.

ROGER: Why not?

MIRANDA: We just can't Roger . . . we're too different . . .

ROGER: Different? How?

MIRANDA: Oh in a hundred ways . . . I mean, for a start I'm a woman and you're . . . you're a *man* . . .

ROGER: Well, people of the same sex don't get married.

MIRANDA: My fathers did.

ROGER: We'll run away together and start a little shop somewhere and sell things.

MIRANDA: Go into trade?

ROGER (*eyes shining*): Yes! Trade's exciting — it's a challenge . . . I've thought it all over, Miranda . . . that's where the future of our country lies. Buying and selling . . . profit margins . . . cost-effective management . . . sales projections . . . those are *real* . . . those are things that *count!*

MIRANDA (*laying aside her ivory handled hairbrush and standing*): You're mad! You'll own sixteen mansions all over the world when your father dies, and yet you want to throw it all up and go into trade!

ROGER (*following her*): Don't you see it? It's beautiful! Suppose I buy six dozen gross of elastic stocking hose — I'm thinking of a chemists' sundries shop — at two shillings a dozen . . . I sell them for four shillings a dozen — that's a gross profit of twelve shillings per dozen . . . allow a shilling for overheads — transport, wages, heating — that's eleven shillings clear profit . . .

ROGER pauses expectantly . . . breathless with excitement. His eyes shining.

The beautiful and slightly mysterious MIRANDA frowns.

MIRANDA: That's *net* profit is it?
ROGER: Yes.

MIRANDA turns away, preoccupied with her own thoughts.

MIRANDA *(wilfully)*: Supposing one stocked a herbal remedy . . .
ROGER *(cautioningly)*: Not the kind you need a prescription for?
MIRANDA: Obviously not . . . a herbal remedy in gallon cans and dispensed it in two-ounce bottles at the same price. What percentage return would that mean?

ROGER stops close behind her, his eyes glistening.

ROGER: You're talking of a profit margin of . . . two thousand per cent!
MIRANDA *(her lips part and her heart races a little)*: Oh . . . but we couldn't do that . . .
ROGER: Why not? We can do anything!
MIRANDA *(her voice husky with passion)*: We could sell . . . toilet requisites . . .
ROGER: And shaving accessories . . .
MIRANDA: And douches! We could sell douches . . .
ROGER: Oh, Miranda . . . say yes.

MIRANDA hesitates — her eyes aglow. Suddenly she turns away.

MIRANDA: No, no, Roger . . . I can't . . .
ROGER: But Miranda! *(He takes her by the arm.)*
MIRANDA: No no no, Roger — we're too rich! Don't you understand?
ROGER: We could have a surgical goods section as well . . .
MIRANDA *(anguished)*: No, Roger . . . we must have country houses, and croquet parties and grouse shoots . . . you know that . . .
ROGER: Why?
MIRANDA: Someone has to, Roger.
ROGER: Miranda . . .
MIRANDA: No, please, I can hear Father. You *must* go. He's terribly rich!

ROGER, after a moment's brave indecision, rushes to the window, and makes his escape.

A few days later.
Once again it is breakfast time. The only discernible difference from Bartlesham Hall is that the servant dealing with the silver trays of food is Indian. LORD *and* LADY BARTLESHAM *sit at either end of the long table, as usual.* ROGER *sits despondently in the middle, toying with his food. Four large uneaten platefuls of cornflakes and kidneys surround him.*

LORD BARTLESHAM *lays aside the* Times of India *for a moment and looks up reflectively.*

LORD BARTLESHAM:	You know they're extraordinary people . . . the Pathans . . .
LADY BARTLESHAM:	Who? Derek and Edna?
LORD BARTLESHAM:	No — the Pathans . . . the local tribe we're fighting . . .
LADY BARTLESHAM	(*losing interest*): Oh yes . . .
LORD BARTLESHAM:	They respond amazingly well to kindness . . .
LADY BARTLESHAM	(*unimpressed*): Hmm.
LORD BARTLESHAM:	They may be very violent, often cruel and senselessly vindictive, but if you're kind to them, they respect you in a strange . . . way . . . Jellicoe was telling me of a chap who was kind to them . . . they wouldn't leave him alone — slept outside his door every night . . .
LADY BARTLESHAM:	Really?
LORD BARTLESHAM:	Mind you, he was *very* kind to them . . .
LADY BARTLESHAM:	Have you tried the Oxshott Cherry Preserve?
LORD BARTLESHAM:	You know, I often think that if people had been a little more kind to each other, we could have avoided many of the wars which have plagued society through the ages . . .
LADY BARTLESHAM:	Rubbish, dear.
LORD BARTLESHAM:	Well . . . maybe . . . but just suppose for a minute that when Wallenstein reached the gates of Magdeburg in 1631, instead of razing the city to the ground and putting its inhabitants to the sword, he'd said . . . 'What a lovely place! How lucky you are to live here . . . I live in Sweden . . . you must come and see me some time' . . . Just think what a difference it would have made . . . he'd have gone down in history as a nice chap, instead of the Butcher of Magdeburg . . .
LADY BARTLESHAM:	Eat up dear, and stop talking piffle.

ROGER looks up. His eyes widen, for at the window he can see the
HONOURABLE MIRANDA. She signals to him and disappears.

ROGER pushes his chair back noisily and stands up.

LADY BARTLESHAM:	Where are you going, Roger?
ROGER:	To see Mr Hopper.
LADY BARTLESHAM:	There are eight more courses yet . . .
ROGER:	We're doing Horace today.
LORD BARTLESHAM	(*looking up from his paper*): Child molester, wasn't he?
LADY BARTLESHAM:	(*impatiently*): No . . . no . . . Horace is a Latin author, Barty.

ROGER makes good his escape.

LORD BARTLESHAM:	Knew a child molester at Eton called Horace.
LADY BARTLESHAM	(*looking round at the door after ROGER*): I don't know what's come over the boy, I really don't. He's been off his kedgeree for weeks.
LORD BARTLESHAM:	Perhaps we should have given him more love and affection . . .
LADY BARTLESHAM:	More brute force, if you ask me — like we did with Nigel.
LORD BARTLESHAM:	Nigel died.
LADY BARTLESHAM:	Yes, but think what he'd have been like if he'd lived!

Out in the garden, ROGER appears looking around for the HONOURABLE
MIRANDA.

An Indian servant watches him disapprovingly.

Suddenly he hears a 'Pssst!' and sees MIRANDA behind an urn on the lawn,
beckoning him over.

ROGER:	Miranda! What is it?
MIRANDA:	I've decided to come with you.
ROGER	(*slightly nonplussed*): Where?
MIRANDA:	I've bought the option on a two-floor lock-up in the Euston Road . . . complete with stock.
ROGER	(*in some alarm*): But I'm not ready!
MIRANDA:	It's haberdashery mainly, but we could open an accessories section and move into surgical appliances when we've built the business up.
ROGER	(*excited but alarmed*): Look, Miranda . . . I . . .
MIRANDA:	I'll call for you tonight. I'll bring Rover.

MIRANDA gives him a neck-breaking kiss and disappears.

ROGER is left incredulous. Suddenly it's all happening for him.

Nightfall finds ROGER sitting, fully dressed, on the edge of his bed, waiting.
His excited face illuminated by the pale rays of the moon.

That night I waited, ready . . . ready for the chance of a lifetime. This time it *had* to work . . .

Suddenly there is the sound of gravel being thrown at the window.

ROGER starts. His hands tighten on his bundle of clothes and he moves towards the window. He opens it.

A ladder has been set against the wall, but coming up the ladder is not the dainty sylph-like form of his beloved, but the hairy-faced, Russian-hatted figure of HOPPER.

HOPPER is armed to the teeth, and has a carbine slung over his back. He's pulling behind him a formidable bundle of weapons tied together on the end of a rope.

ROGER: Mr Hopper!

HOPPER looks up, his eyes are shining and he is clearly excited.

HOPPER: Roger . . . you heard the news then?
ROGER: What news?
HOPPER: The Tsar of all the Russias is dead — isn't it wonderful?
ROGER: Well . . . yes of course . . .

HOPPER has climbed in by now, he pulls the weapons after him.

82

HOPPER: Russia's up in arms. The Revolution's begun . . . (*He points to the pile of arms.*) . . . stack that lot in your room, Roger . . .

HOPPER turns and starts to haul up yet another load of small arms and machine guns.

ROGER: Mr Hopper . . . I'm leaving.

HOPPER: No need! We'll start our uprising here! The entire regiment's with us . . . the armed struggle of the proletariat has begun! Today — the Empire! Tomorrow . . . England itself!

ROGER: I can't, Mr Hopper.

HOPPER: What? (*He stops hauling in the next load.*)

ROGER: The Honourable Miranda and I are going back home to start a little shop.

HOPPER: But I need you for the coup . . .

ROGER: I'm sorry, Mr Hopper . . .

ROGER starts to go into the corridor.

HOPPER makes towards him . . . as he does so he lets go of the rope.

There is an almighty crash of arms hitting the drive below.

The sound carries as far as LORD *and* LADY BARTLESHAM's *bedroom.* LORD BARTLESHAM *sits bolt upright.*

LORD BARTLESHAM: The Pathans!

LADY BARTLESHAM: Derek and Edna?

LORD BARTLESHAM: No — the violent but proud race of hill people who threaten our very existence. I must go and be kind to them.

LADY BARTLESHAM: Don't be silly, dear. The servants have orders to come and tell us if there's a Pathan uprising.

Meanwhile, out on the landing, ROGER *is backing away from* HOPPER, *who is now advancing menacingly towards him.*

HOPPER: I spent fourteen years teaching you . . . training you for this moment . . . You can't walk out on me now, d'you hear?

ROGER: 'No man owns another,' Mr Hopper.

HOPPER grabs ROGER and flattens him against the wall.

ROGER kicks HOPPER, and slips out of his grasp, and then races down the corridor towards his bedroom door.

Whereupon HOPPER picks up a rifle and takes aim.

HOPPER (*in a hissed whisper*): Stay where you are! You'll do as I say. Now turn around.

ROGER *slowly turns round, as he does so he grabs a vase, perched on a conveniently high stand, and flings it at* HOPPER, *throwing himself to the floor.*

HOPPER *fires wildly.*

Back in Lord and Lady Bartlesham's bedroom the shot is still echoing. LORD BARTLESHAM *sits up in bed again.*

LORD BARTLESHAM: My God! They're armed!
LADY BARTLESHAM: Nonsense, dear . . . it's probably just Mr Muckbee shooting an intruder . . .
LORD BARTLESHAM: I'd better go and treat them well.
LADY BARTLESHAM (*firmly*): Lie down and go to sleep.

They lie down. There is another gunshot and another.

LADY BARTLESHAM: Probably shooting the intruder's family as well . . . I don't know *why* they bring them with them . . .

By now ROGER *has managed to get back into his own room. He slams the door behind him and locks it.*

HOPPER *starts rattling the handle.*

ROGER *looks around for his clothes, grabs a few, and runs for the window. It is stuck.*

HOPPER (*loud whisper*): Roger, listen . . . I want you to *lead* the Revolution.
ROGER (*in an equally loud whisper*): Go away!

HOPPER *batters away at the door and it starts to splinter.*

Back in Lord and Lady Bartlesham's bedroom, the sound of splintering wood is unmistakably audible. LORD BARTLESHAM *sits bolt upright once again.*

LORD BARTLESHAM: They're breaking the place up! They need sympathy . . .

There is another splintering crash.

LADY BARTLESHAM: Don't be silly Barty, go to sleep!
LORD BARTLESHAM   (*rising*): Perhaps I'd better go and check . . . give them all some hot soup and blankets . . . make them full members of the Club . . .

He reaches for his dressing gown.

In the meantime ROGER *has succeeded in opening the window. He climbs out onto the roof of the verandah and drops down, landing spectacularly.*

At this moment, HOPPER *finally bursts into the room.*

He dashes to the window, looks out and takes aim and fires.

ROGER *sprints across the gravel driveway into the bushes. Under this cover he starts to make his way towards the gates, where the* HONOURABLE MIRANDA *has just arrived.*

His escape is cut short, however, when he parts some bushes, and comes face to face with a huddle of officers from his father's Regiment.

FIRST OFFICER: Ah, there you are, sir. Mr Hopper told us to wait here for you.

ROGER: Look . . . I'm not in all this.

FIRST OFFICER: What do you reckon now, sir? Do we wait for Mr Hopper?

ROGER: Look, it's no good asking me . . . I'm off to start a little shop somewhere, with —

The OFFICER slaps a hand over ROGER's mouth and pulls him to one side, looking round anxiously at the bushes behind him.

FIRST OFFICER: Look sir . . . the men are expecting you to lead them. You can't let them down now . . .

ROGER becomes aware of the rest of the Regiment, armed to the teeth, and crouching in the bushes behind.

ROGER: I can't help that. (*He starts to go.*)

There is a click.

The FIRST OFFICER produces a loaded revolver and points it at him.

FIRST OFFICER: I'm sorry sir, but you'd better do just as I say.

There is another shot from the house. They all look up.

Back in ROGER's bedroom.

HOPPER has just fired again, when LORD BARTLESHAM bursts in, holding a tray with some drinks on.

LORD BARTLESHAM: Hello Pathans! How about a drink and some hot sou— Good Lord! Hopper . . .

HOPPER looks distinctly uncomfortable being caught at a window with a smoking rifle and wearing a complete Russian outfit.

LORD BARTLESHAM: You haven't killed any of them, have you?

HOPPER (*confused*): What sir?

LORD BARTLESHAM: The Pathans . . .

HOPPER: It's not the Pathans sir . . . it's . . . it's your own men.

LORD BARTLESHAM: Disguised as Pathans?

HOPPER: No, no, your own men are firing.

LORD BARTLESHAM: You mean . . . like in a mutiny, Hopper?

HOPPER (*takes a big breath — this is the moment of truth*): Yes, sir! I'm afraid this *is* a mutiny.

HOPPER *points his rifle at* LORD BARTLESHAM *in a vaguely coercive manner.*

LORD BARTLESHAM: Thank God you're still with me, Hopper.
HOPPER: Er no . . . no . . . I'm . . .

LORD BARTLESHAM *walks past* HOPPER, *not noticing the rifle, and giving him a reassuring pat on the shoulder.*

LORD BARTLESHAM: The wife and I always had a soft spot for you. (*He peers out of window.*)
HOPPER: Look, I've . . . er . . . I'm . . .

HOPPER *tries to bring himself to point the rifle at* LORD BARTLESHAM *but the old man is awkwardly close.*

LORD BARTLESHAM (*scanning the bushes*): What do they want? Money? Double beds? Who the hell's behind this?
HOPPER: Sir . . . (*Swallows.*) I have to tell you . . .

LORD BARTLESHAM *turns and peers closely into* HOPPER's *face . . . obviously intrigued by the tension in* HOPPER's *voice . . .*

LORD BARTLESHAM: What?

HOPPER *cannot stand the close eye-contact with his patron of twenty years.*

HOPPER: Er . . . I have to tell you . . . it's your son.
LORD BARTLESHAM: They've got him too?

LORD BARTLESHAM *grabs the rifle and aims out of the window.*

HOPPER: No . . . he's leading them, sir . . .

LORD BARTLESHAM *freezes, lowers the rifle and pulls it back into the room.*

He slowly turns to HOPPER, *very subdued.*

LORD BARTLESHAM: My son? Leading a mutiny?
HOPPER: I'm afraid so.
LORD BARTLESHAM: You mean . . . little .. . little what's his name?
HOPPER (*now sold on shopping* ROGER): Thingy . . . yes . . . He's the ringleader.

LORD BARTLESHAM *is thunderstruck.*

LORD BARTLESHAM: But *why?* We gave the dear boy everything. A good home . . . several good homes — initialled croquet mallets, hand-tooled books on etiquette . . . What more does he want?
HOPPER (*can't resist the opportunity*): Perhaps he wants to found a Socialist State with centralized ownership of capital to be used for the benefit of all.
LORD BARTLESHAM: He wants *what?*

HOPPER *is a little terrified but decides to brave it out.*

HOPPER: A . . . a . . . Socialist State with centralized ownership of capital to be used for the benefit of all . . . your lordship.
LORD BARTLESHAM: Oh . . . if that's all he wants he shall have it.
HOPPER (*taken off guard*): I'm sorry?
LORD BARTLESHAM: No son of mine shall ever want for anything, Hopper.
HOPPER: Oh . . . (*with dawning realization.*) . . . *Oh!* Ah . . . Ah well . . .

LADY BARTLESHAM *appears.*

LADY BARTLESHAM: What's going on, Barty?
LORD BARTLESHAM: Boy wants the centralized ownership of capital to be used for the benefit of all, dear.
LADY BARTLESHAM: The ungrateful little bastard!

LADY BARTLESHAM *grabs the rifle and gives it an automatic and professional examination, cocking it as she does so.*

Meanwhile, at the gates, the HONOURABLE MIRANDA *can bear the tension no longer.*

MIRANDA: I'm going to find out what's happening. Wait for me here, Rover.

Her Indian serving-lady nods obediently.

MIRANDA makes her way through the garden. She sees the lights on in the big house through the trees.

Suddenly she freezes as she sees the group of mutinous soldiers, with ROGER at their head.

FIRST OFFICER (*to ROGER*): Tell them the place is surrounded and that you are taking over personal command.

ROGER: Look, I really . . .

The FIRST OFFICER cocks his pistol.

ROGER realizes he means business, and allows himself to be pushed forward into the driveway. He walks warily towards the house.

ROGER: Hello . . .

LADY BARTLESHAM takes careful aim.

LADY BARTLESHAM: There he is now. One shot and we can all go back to bed.
ROGER: Can everybody hear me?
LORD BARTLESHAM: Perhaps we should just hear what he has to say, dear.
LADY BARTLESHAM: This is no time to be sentimental, Barty. We do have other children.

ROGER's voice rises up from below. It sounds more plaintive than threatening.

ROGER: It is important you listen carefully . . . er . . . to everything I say . . . er . . . and act accordingly . . .

The mutinous soldiers train their guns on his head, their fingers squeezing

90

slightly on the triggers.

Roger's mother follows suit.

Meanwhile, the HONOURABLE MIRANDA *has edged her way up behind the soldiers. She reaches down and picks up a heavy stick.*

ROGER: The house . . . is surrounded . . . and I am taking personal command of the Regiment . . .

For the first time, it is LORD BARTLESHAM's *turn to be outraged.*

LORD BARTLESHAM: Good Lord — *my* Regiment! Give me that!

He makes a grab for the rifle, but LADY BARTLESHAM *hangs on to it.*

LADY BARTLESHAM: Oh Barty, leave it to me.

Meanwhile ROGER *is biting his lip, but carrying on bravely, if a trifle quietly.*

ROGER: This is at the insistence of the officers and men of the Regiment. (*He hears the noise of a scuffle at the window as* LADY BARTLESHAM *and* LORD

BARTLESHAM *argue.*) Though . . . I must point out I'm doing this under duress . . .

In the bushes, fingers tighten on the triggers and gunsights are retrained on his slight figure.

ROGER: Despite my high regard for the ideals of the men.

The FIRST OFFICER *however, raises his hand for them to wait. Meanwhile,* MIRANDA *closes in on the hindmost soldiers.*

Suddenly ROGER *turns towards the soldiers in the bushes.*

ROGER: But I would say to them first of all that obviously Mr Hopper has been talking revolution to you as he has talked revolution to me for the last fifteen years of Latin classes . . .

LORD and LADY BARTLESHAM stop fighting for a moment and turn on HOPPER.

HOPPER smiles hopelessly, as ROGER continues to spill his beans.

ROGER: And no doubt, when I've taken over command of the Regiment, Mr Hopper will expect to take over ultimate power through me . . .

At this, the mutineers look at each other with slightly furrowed brows.

ROGER   (*gaining a little confidence*): So I ask the officers and men of the Regiment, what will they have achieved? They will have substituted one figure of authority for another.

The soldiers frown behind their rifles.

What guarantee have they that Mr Hopper — or I for that matter — will treat them any better than my father?

The political tenor of ROGER's train of thought, however, has got HOPPER really agitated, and he cannot stop himself yelling out of the window.

HOPPER: Don't listen to him! That's not Marxism. That's Bakuninite Anarchism..

LORD and LADY BARTLESHAM are looking at HOPPER in a new light, but MR HOPPER is so incensed by ROGER's unorthodoxy that he has forgotten all about his former patrons. He makes to grab the rifle from LORD BARTLESHAM.

Meanwhile ROGER is getting carried away with his own oratory.

ROGER: So I say, let us grasp this opportunity to renounce the violence implicit in

any centralized authority, and aim for a total decentralization of power!

Several of the soldiers have trouble trying to keep up with this change of political direction.

HOPPER however, has no doubts. He has grabbed the rifle and is now aiming it at ROGER.

HOPPER: Anarchist!

At this moment MIRANDA looms up behind one of the hindmost soldiers. She clubs him (rather effectively for such a delicate beauty) and takes his rifle.

The FIRST OFFICER runs out from the bushes.

FIRST OFFICER: Listen! He's got our position slightly wrong. We're not *against* a centralized authority as such . . .

SECOND OFFICER: (*from the bushes*): I am!

FIRST OFFICER: No you're not!

ANOTHER VOICE   (*from the bushes*): I agree with the last speaker.

HOPPER: This isn't a bloody debate! It's time for action.

LORD BARTLESHAM makes a grab for the rifle and they wrestle.

MIRANDA *has climbed into the branches of a tree, she produces a rifle, takes aim and fires at the window from which* HOPPER *is shouting. She extinguishes the lamp within, with expert marksmanship.*

HOPPER *and* LORD *and* LADY BARTLESHAM *still continue to struggle in the dark. The rifle goes off.*

ROGER *ducks as the bullet whistles past his head and dodges behind a stone urn.*

FIRST OFFICER VOICE (*panicked by the gunfire*): Fire!
(*from bushes, by now extremely confused*): Who at?

MIRANDA *fires again. Another light goes out in the house.*

HOPPER *fires back, as bullets hit the window frame around him.*

Suddenly LADY BARTLESHAM *re-appears at the door of the room carrying a machine gun.*

LADY BARTLESHAM (*joyfully*): Look what I've found!

A bullet smashes through the window.

All this time ROGER *is cowering behind the urn.*

MIRANDA, *however, coolly fires at another light.*

A soldier wheels round to fire at MIRANDA *in the tree.*

LADY BARTLESHAM *looking as happy as she ever will be, rakes the grounds indiscriminately with machine gun fire.*

The mutinous soldiers whirl round in confusion and fling themselves to the ground.

FIRST OFFICER: Charge!
SECOND OFFICER: Which way?
ANOTHER: Where are we?

MIRANDA fires and puts out yet another light.

LADY BARTLESHAM turns the machine gun towards her and fires, raking her tree and knocking the rifle from her hands.

ROGER notices MIRANDA for the first time.

ROGER (*shouts*): Miranda!
MIRANDA: I'm coming! . . . Rover!

The Indian lady pricks up her ears, does a great leap on to the back of the horse leading the trap and whips it furiously. The trap speeds off up the garden drive into the maelstrom of bullets and noise.

As the trap speeds past the urn, the Indian lady leans down from the horse and scoops ROGER up with an Errol-Flynnish flourish.

They career on round the drive and as they come to the other gates, pass under the tree where MIRANDA has been perched, she drops down into the trap and they speed off into the night, leaving chaos behind them, shouting and firing.

The trap hurtles away down the moonlit track.

Exactly what happened that night in India will probably never be known, for no one lived to tell the tale save myself and the Honourable Miranda. After many adventures we found our way back to England, and there we achieved our impossible dream . . .

Outside an old-fashioned chemist's shop hangs a sign which reads:

'Lord Bartlesham and the Honourable Miranda Fyffe-Moncrieff, Duchess of Lincoln: Chemists' sundries, accessories, douches a speciality'

Outside stand the proud owners — ROGER *and* MIRANDA.

. . . To be able to throw off the shackles of wealth and privilege, and live as we'd always wanted to live, as simple shopkeepers . . .

It is noticeable, however, that the shop is actually built on to the imposing front entrance of Bartlesham Hall. And so, as music swells in our ears, we leave ROGER *and his bride happy at last — with Bartlesham Hall and its gardens in all their splendour — undiminished.*

THE END